Universal Healthcare without the NHS

This publication is based on research that forms part of the Paragon Initiative.

This five-year project will provide a fundamental reassessment of what government should – and should not – do. It will put every area of government activity under the microscope and analyse the failure of current policies.

The project will put forward clear and considered solutions to the UK's problems. It will also identify the areas of government activity that can be put back into the hands of individuals, families, civil society, local government, charities and markets.

The Paragon Initiative will create a blueprint for a better, freer Britain – and provide a clear vision of a new relationship between the state and society.

This publication was made possible through the support of a grant from the John Templeton Foundation and complementary funding from the Age Endeavour Fellowship.

The opinions expressed in this publication are those of the author and do not necessarily reflect the views of the John Templeton Foundation or the Age Endeavour Fellowship.

UNIVERSAL HEALTHCARE WITHOUT THE NHS

Towards a Patient-Centred Health System

KRISTIAN NIEMIETZ

First published in Great Britain in 2016 by
The Institute of Economic Affairs
2 Lord North Street
Westminster
London SW1P 3LB
in association with London Publishing Partnership Ltd
www.londonpublishingpartnership.co.uk

The mission of the Institute of Economic Affairs is to improve understanding
of the fundamental institutions of a free society by analysing and expounding
the role of markets in solving economic and social problems.

A CIP catalogue record for this book is available from the British Library.

ISBN 978-0-255-36737-0

Many IEA publications are translated into languages other
than English or are reprinted. Permission to translate or to reprint
should be sought from the Director General at the address above.

Typeset in Kepler by T&T Productions Ltd
www.tandtproductions.com

Printed and bound in Great Britain by Hobbs the Printers Ltd

CONTENTS

THE AUTHOR

Dr Kristian Niemietz is the Head of Health and Welfare at the Institute of Economic Affairs, and a Research Fellow at the Age Endeavour Fellowship (AEF). Kristian studied economics at the Humboldt-Universität zu Berlin and the Universidad de Salamanca, and political economy at King's College London, where he obtained his doctorate.

He is the author of the IEA monographs *Redefining the Poverty Debate* and *A New Understanding of Poverty*, the latter winning the 2011 Templeton Freedom Award in the category 'Free Enterprise Solutions to Poverty'.

FOREWORD

Nigel Lawson famously said: 'The NHS is the closest thing the English people have now to a religion'. For a long time this stubborn fact enraged only the Conservative Party. Tony Blair came to rue this same fact once his Labour government started to introduce choice-based market mechanisms in order to increase both quality and efficiency in the health service. The deep-seated public faith in the NHS enrages many – on left and right – who have a broader experience of health systems and a deeper knowledge of the facts. The NHS is not the 'envy of the world', as is commonly asserted. Need proof? It has never been copied outside the shores of the UK.

This leads to periodic attempts to set the record straight and thereby bring the public to their senses. Kristian Niemietz's excellent book is just the latest of these. Unfortunately, just as regularly as academics, strategists and polemicists – and Kristian Niemietz is a stirring mixture of all three – have sallied forth, so they have come undone. Why? Facts and arguments don't matter when it comes to the NHS – only emotion and sentiment register. Commentators often talk about us living in a 'post-fact' world. If that is so the NHS led the way – debate about its future has been conducted in post-factual terms for quite some time.

Just take the two most recent disputes. There were claims that the proposed Transatlantic Trade and Investment Partnership (TTIP) between the US and the EU would lead to forced privatisation of the NHS. Of course, it would do nothing of the sort – it is merely a bigger, bolder version of the 'privatisation myth'. The second recent row relates to the claim, often touted by Labour Party opposition frontbenchers, that the Tory government is intent on privatising the health service. The proportion of spend that is actually put out to tender is small and anyway all contracts come back again – no services are alienated. More importantly, one of the most loved parts of the NHS is primary care – and what are GPs? GPs are private providers who contract to the NHS just like BUPA or Virgin or Kaiser Permanente. It's just that GPs chose to sort out their contracting arrangements nearly 70 years ago, so they feel like part of the fabric of the NHS.

What should rational people who care about the quality of healthcare in Britain and who want patients here to get a service as good as the best in France, Germany or Australia do about this apparent stand-off between facts and emotions? In the words of Yogi Berra, the legendary baseball player, coach and manager: 'When you come to a fork in the road, take it.' Seize the facts and the emotions and build on both – refuse to allow them to become an opposition.

Niemietz rightly reminds us of the prehistory of the NHS, the rich roots in mutualism and municipalism. That history is a resource for reminding us that non-state provision is not alien to the UK. In a similar way we have the many struggles of minority ethnic communities through voluntary and community organisations to get issues such as thalassemia and sickle cell disease on the agenda of the mainstream NHS. Monopoly provision all too easily leads to a monopoly mentality – 'sod the customer', as Kingsley Amis put it.

Kristian Niemietz wields the evidence on international comparisons carefully – though the desire to prove the NHS is not as good as voters think it is is pretty apparent. That desire to prove the patient wrong is, in the end, the fatal flaw of reformers. The facts on their own aren't a spur for action but a source of stubborn support. In a cage match, emotion always triumphs over fact. Look rather to the subtle approach of NHS Chief Executive Simon Stevens. He has said, and like any good message transmitter repeats frequently, that obesity is the new smoking. What is the policy response? Lectures and admonitions? No, an equally often repeated desire to turn the NHS from a public service into a public movement. Mobilise all that passion and emotion and channel it away from fighting against closures and turn it towards personal and collective transformation.

Anyone who has thought hard about the NHS knows that it faces challenges and needs to change. The policy will be contested but at base the politics are simple. A society that is growing richer – as ours is – will naturally spend more money on services such as health and education. The only questions, at base, are how that money is raised – publicly or privately – and how that money is best spent to buy improvements in health. As Ronald Reagan used to say, 'It's not easy, but it is simple.' A debate is raging among experts about how we strike the balance. Kristian Niemietz has made the best kind of contribution to that debate – sharp, well-researched and well-written.

JOHN MCTERNAN
Head, International Political at Penn Schoen Berland
October 2016

SUMMARY

- Despite some relative improvements in the last fifteen years, the National Health Service remains an international laggard in terms of those health outcomes that can be attributed to the healthcare system. In international comparisons of health system performance, the NHS almost always ranks in the bottom third, on a par with the Czech Republic and Slovenia. In a 'blind test', in which we look at health outcome data, and guess which data point represents which country, the UK could easily be mistaken for an Eastern European country. We would certainly never mistake the UK for Switzerland or Belgium.
- Age-standardised survival rates for the most common types of cancer remain several percentage points below rates achieved in most other developed countries, and such differences translate into thousands of lives lost. For example, if the UK's breast cancer, prostate cancer, lung cancer and bowel cancer patients were treated in the Netherlands rather than on the NHS, more than 9,000 lives would be saved every year. If they were treated in Germany, more than 12,000 lives would be saved, and if they were treated in Belgium, more than 14,000 lives would be saved. A similar picture emerges for a range of other conditions, as well as for more holistic measures of health system performance. For example, the UK has one of the highest rates of avoidable deaths in Western Europe. If this rate were cut to the levels observed in Belgium, more than 10,000 lives would be saved every year. More than 13,000 lives would be saved if the rate were cut to Dutch levels.

- The one study which seemingly comes to a radically different conclusion is the Commonwealth Fund study, which ranks the NHS as the world's top performer. Illustrating the dynamics of confirmation bias, the Commonwealth Fund study has therefore acquired the status of a trump card in the British healthcare debate. However, there is only one category in the Commonwealth Fund study which looks at health outcomes, and in that category, the NHS ranks, once again, second to last. Thus, even the preferred study of NHS supporters shows that the NHS is an international laggard in terms of outcomes.

- The UK spends less on healthcare than many other developed countries, but this must not be mistaken for a sign of superior efficiency. It is mostly the result of crude rationing: innovative medicines and therapies that are routinely available in other high-income countries are often hard to come by in the UK. Any country could keep healthcare spending in check by simply refusing to adopt medical innovation. In more sophisticated estimates of health system efficiency, the NHS ranks, once again, in the bottom third.

- The NHS is poorly prepared to deal with the financial challenges of an ageing society. This is because, like virtually all health systems in the developed world, it is financed on a pay-as-you-go basis: healthcare costs rise systematically with age, which is why most healthcare spending represents a transfer from the working-age generation to the retired generation. Increasing longevity and low birth rates therefore represent a pincer movement which threatens the system's financial viability. The fundamental problem is that the NHS (like other health systems) lacks old-age reserves. It should have started building up an old-age reserve fund, analogous to a pension fund, decades ago.

- While NHS performance looks unimpressive in snapshot cross-country comparisons, it does better on time series.

Compared to the 1990s, the NHS has improved both in absolute terms and relative to its peers.

- Its critics sometimes compare the NHS to a 'Soviet style' state monolith: this characterisation is no longer accurate (if it ever was). There have been two major attempts to introduce market mechanisms into the NHS. The first attempt, the 'internal market' of the 1990s, did not succeed: the NHS was not yet ready for competition at the time. Important preconditions were lacking, in particular, there was a severe dearth of information about provider performance and quality of care. The second attempt, the 'quasi-market' of the 2000s, was a qualified success, because this time the preconditions had already been established.

- In other policy debates, there is willingness to learn from international best practice, and a general curiosity about successful models abroad. English free schools, for example, were modelled on the Swedish friskolor. Healthcare is the exception to this rule. The healthcare debate remains insular and inward-looking, blighted by a counterproductive tendency to pretend that the only conceivable alternative to the NHS is the American system.

- It would be far more insightful to benchmark the NHS against social health insurance (SHI) systems, the model of healthcare adopted by Switzerland, Belgium, the Netherlands, Germany and Israel. Like the NHS, SHI systems also achieve universal access to healthcare, albeit in a different way, namely through a combination of means-tested insurance premium subsidies, community rating and risk structure compensation. Unlike in the US, there is therefore no uninsured population (even homeless people have health insurance), and there is no such thing as a 'medical bankruptcy'. When it comes to providing high-quality healthcare to the poor, these systems are second to none: in this respect, there is nothing the

NHS has achieved which the SHI systems have not also achieved.

- In terms of outcomes, quality and efficiency, social health insurance systems are consistently ahead of the NHS on almost every available measure. They combine the universality of a public system with the consumer sovereignty, the pluralism, the competitiveness and the innovativeness of a market system. We do not see any one particular country's health system as a role model, because they all have flaws and irritating aspects of their own. But there are also plenty of interesting lessons to be learned, which we are missing out on by ignoring alternatives to both the NHS and the American system.

- The Dutch system shows that a successful health system needs no state-owned hospitals, no state hospital planning and no hospital subsidies. The Swiss system shows that even substantial levels of out-of-pocket patient charges need not be regressive, and that people can be trusted to choose sensibly from a variety of health insurance plans. The 'PKV-pillar' of the German system shows that a healthcare system can be fully prefunded, just like a pension system.

- The quasi-market reforms of the 2000s can be built upon, to move gradually from the status quo to a pluralistic, consumer-oriented healthcare system. Clinical Commissioning Groups (CCGs) are, in a sense, comparable to insurers, so giving people free choice of CCG would be a necessary (albeit not sufficient) first step towards creating a quasi-SHI system. CCGs' budgets would then have to correspond closely to the risk profile of the patient population they cover, and this market should also be opened to private non-profit and for-profit insurers. CCGs and non-NHS insurers should be free to offer a variety of health plans, including plans with co-payments and deductibles in exchange for rebates.

TABLES, FIGURES AND BOXES

1 AN ALTERNATIVE HISTORY: WHAT BRITAIN WOULD HAVE BEEN LIKE WITHOUT THE NHS

In a universe not far from our own

The announcement by the 'Big Eight', the UK's major health insurance groups, to raise premiums faster than the rate of inflation for the sixth year in succession has sparked angry responses from across the political spectrum. The Secretary of State for Health called the decision a 'disgrace' and an 'affront to hard-working families up and down the country'. The prime minister concurred, and renewed her pledge to tackle the issue of rising healthcare costs during this parliament.

Several measures are already in preparation. They include a 'naming-and-shaming list', in which health insurers and healthcare providers have to disclose all bonus payments exceeding a certain threshold. The Department of Health is also reviewing plans to give the healthcare regulator, OfHealth, greater powers to shape the tariff structure and pricing policy of healthcare companies. Since the beginning of this year, health insurers are already obliged to inform consumers regularly about the existence of cheaper tariffs, and about how much money they could save by changing health plans. The government has also launched a public awareness campaign, SwitchHealth, to encourage price comparisons between insurers and increase switching rates. In addition, the prime minister has recently announced her intention to reform the corporate governance of the health sector. Patients are to be represented on the company boards of insurers and healthcare groups, and all foreign takeovers of companies above a certain size are going to be subject to a 'public interest test'. The Chancellor, meanwhile, has hinted at the possibility of making the tax advantages enjoyed by the health industry conditional on stable or falling premiums.

Industry representatives have dismissed public anger over industry profits as 'obsessive' and 'misguided'. They claim that neither their profit rates nor their levels of executive remuneration are any higher than in comparable industries, and that both had been flatlining for a long time anyway. They also claim that prices in the non-profit sector are, on average, the same as in the for-profit sector. They cite increased costs, especially the new obligation to include the newest generation of cancer drugs in the standard health benefits package, as the reason for the increase in premiums.

But then, they would say that. Their objections are unlikely to go down well with the British public, who take an increasingly critical view of the healthcare industry. According to the latest British Social Attitudes survey, more than four out of five people support a government-mandated five-year premium freeze, and about three in four support a permanent absolute cap, under which premiums can only be raised in line with inflation. About as many support banning bonus payments altogether, and almost as many support a statutory maximum wage for health industry executives. Price controls for pharmaceuticals and medical equipment also enjoy high levels of popular support.

Perhaps strangely, then, the opposition leader's plans to nationalise most of the health insurance industry, together with the large hospital and managed care groups, do not find much resonance with the public. According to the latest IpsosMORI poll, fewer than one in four people support this option. Qualitative research by the Institute for Social and Economic Research (ISER) echoes those findings. As one participant in their focus group interviews put it:

Of course there are problems with the current system, and it needs reform. We all know that. But do we seriously want politicians and bureaucrats to be in charge of our health? That's just absurd. What's next, state-run breweries and bakeries? No, we need to quit this habit of shouting 'nationalise it' whenever something doesn't quite work the way we want it too.

Healthcare is an outlier in this respect. In other sectors, calls for industry nationalisations are usually popular. Whether it is energy companies, railways, banks, postal services – one can pick almost any industry at random and safely bet that at least two out of three people will want to see it nationalised.[1] As journalist Ian Dunt puts it: 'the public hardly believe in the private running of anything'.[2] But they do not seem to trust politicians with their health. In the UK, the idea of state-run healthcare is politically beyond the pale. Even Tony Benn and Michael Foot never called for a wholesale nationalisation of the sector. Why?

'Health systems are characterised by an extremely high degree of status quo bias and inertia', explains Professor Henry Brubaker of the Institute for Studies. 'Once you have a health system in place, you are basically stuck with it, whatever that system is. Outside of extreme events, such as wars, revolutions or the collapse of a regime, there are hardly any examples of countries abolishing a health system and replacing it with another.'

If the UK had, through some historical accident, ended up with state-run healthcare, would that system now be equally immune to fundamental change? It is at least a possibility, and while it is not widely remembered, it is worth pointing out that between 1946 and 1948, there actually was a genuine attempt at

---

1   These survey results are not fictional (see http://www.cityam.com/article/1383618 852/there-sadly-masssupport-nationalisation-and-price-controls).

2   See http://www.politics.co.uk/comment-analysis/2015/09/15/the-questions-corb yn-s-critics-must-answer

a government takeover of the health sector. Under different circumstances, it may well have happened.

In the immediate aftermath of World War II, there was unanimous agreement that the inherited National Health Insurance (NHI) system was in need of serious reform. But there was also 'a noticeable absence of consensus over most basic aspects of health-care policy' (Webster 2002: 3). There were various competing proposals, some of which called for the creation of municipal and/or regional health services, and their most radical variant called for a wholly government-owned and government-run 'national health service'. This latter idea had been around for a while, but it had never really caught on. Even in the early days of the Attlee government, it did not seem to be going anywhere (ibid.: 17):

> The idea of using the Emergency Hospital Service as a springboard for the nationalization of hospitals had been canvassed during the Second World War [...] but this idea had been rejected in all the major planning documents. Although Labour favoured evolution towards a municipal hospital service, its policy statements were careful to avoid offence to the voluntary sector.

But the new health minister Aneurin Bevan was one of the keenest supporters of the idea, and set it on the policy agenda almost single-handedly (ibid.: 14–15):

> [Bevan] struck out in an entirely fresh direction, which placed the emphasis on the scarcely considered alternative of nationalisation. Perhaps within a couple of weeks of his appointment, he was already considering a scheme for bringing all hospitals under a single public authority controlled by the minister [...]
>
> With the aid of his little group of immediate advisers, within a few weeks Bevan had drawn up a firm plan; with little alteration this was translated into legislation within the space of a year. [...]

Although there had been many press leaks concerning Bevan's ideas over the previous six months, it was not until this date [21 March 1946, when the National Health Service Bill was published] that his full intentions became evident.

But once those plans were out in the open, opposition began to form. Parts of the medical profession had been opposed right from the start, but they had little impact: the government dismissed their objections as a selfish defence of their own class interest. On its own, the parliamentary opposition would not have done much to stop the nationalisation plans either. No, what would ultimately stop Bevan's plans was a rift within the organised labour movement itself. The opposition was led by a coalition of Friendly Societies – the working-class mutual insurance associations which had historically provided health insurance for the vast majority of people on modest incomes – and independent hospitals. They realised that the new system would mean the end of working-class mutualism and self-governance, and they had no inclination to become administrators in a state bureaucracy. They were fiercely proud of their autonomy, and they were determined to keep it. They were soon joined by various trade unions, which were running their own independent health insurance schemes for their members as well. A number of professional associations, which also ran health insurance schemes of their own, followed suit.

The general public had never been enthusiastic about Bevan's nationalisation plans anyway. Opinion surveys from the 1930s and 1940s show little enthusiasm for nationalised healthcare (Hayes 2012). Before the autumn of 1946, that reluctance did not translate into active hostility. From then on, however, the anti-nationalisation coalition began to make an impression on the wider public. MPs were bombarded with letters from constituents who opposed the plans, rallies and town hall meetings were held all over the country, and the media coverage of the

Bill turned increasingly negative. Once the organised resistance against the Bill was up and running, the parliamentary opposition jumped on the bandwagon as well, as did detractors within the Parliamentary Labour Party.

It did not help that Bevan utterly failed to understand his critics' position, which he dismissed as parochial and petty-minded. Yet the opponents' case against the Bill was at least as deeply rooted in the labour movement as Bevan's case. They simply reflected two very different conceptions of 'collectivism', between which there had long been a latent conflict, which was now coming to the fore. For one camp, which we might label the 'grassroots collectivists' or 'voluntary collectivists', collectivism simply meant joining forces with others in similar circumstances, and solving problems together, as a group, rather than individually. They believed that in the funding and commissioning of healthcare, group action was generally superior to individual action. But crucially, their version of collectivism had nothing to do with the state. 'The collective' was not the nation as a whole. It was a voluntary, self-organised and self-directed community, usually formed on the basis of shared economic interests and/or a shared social identity.

For the other camp, which we might label the 'paternalist collectivists' or 'national collectivists', the collective was indeed the nation as a whole – opt-outs of individuals or groups who did not want to take part were not to be permitted – and collective provision synonymous with state provision. They believed that the important functions of social and economic life should be taken over by the government, delegated to public sector monopolies and funded on a compulsory basis (national insurance or taxation). More simply put, for the former camp, collectivism meant voluntary communities doing things together, whereas for the second camp, it meant delegating things to the state.

It is difficult to see how a compromise between these two positions could ever have been reached. The two camps simply differed too much in their basic assumptions. To the Bevanites, the 'autonomy' argument made no sense. Like democratic socialists today, the Bevanites did not really think of the state as an actor in its own right. They thought of it as a neutral mechanism, which simply bundled the will of the people, and translated it into action. So they did not think of the planned new health service, or indeed of any nationalised industries, as being run by 'the state' – they thought of them as being run by the people. The state was merely the tool the people used to run things collectively. In this view of the world, the notion that state action could take autonomy away from people must appear absurd.

The manifold problems that we know to beset collective decision-making processes are notably absent from this *Weltanschauung*. Within it there is no such thing as a 'political class' which might have an agenda of its own, no civil service with a potential interest in expanding its own competencies, no interest groups capable of hijacking the political process for their own ends, no 'expressive voting', no 'fiscal illusions', no log-rolling, no horse trading, and so on. The state is assumed to represent 'the people', and when it manifestly does not, this is merely seen as a case for 'trying harder' or electing 'better politicians'.

At the same time, while the Bevanites recognised conflicts of interest between social classes, each social class was thought of as a group with common social and economic interests. The Bevanites saw no qualitative difference between a small, socially homogeneous workers' club, which people could freely join and leave, and 'the working class' as a whole. There was therefore no need for plurality in service provision.

But it was the grassroots collectivists who had the deeper roots within the organised labour movement. Grassroots collectivism was the traditional model of health provision in the UK, especially for working-class people (for the better-off, a combination of private medical insurance and paying out of pocket seemed to work well enough). From the early nineteenth century onwards, workers had begun to organise in Friendly Societies and comparable mutual aid/insurance associations, often built around a workplace or an industry (Green 1985). The number of Friendly Societies expanded throughout the century, as did their membership numbers and the functions they performed. One of their main functions was to pool their members' resources, and to commission medical services and purchase drugs on their behalf. In the field of healthcare, they therefore had two main roles. The first one was the insurance role: they protected their members from the financial risks associated with ill health, by pooling the payment of medical bills, and breaking them down into manageable instalments. The second was the commissioning role: they acted as institutional purchasers, who bundled consumer power, knowledge about healthcare providers, and expertise in contracting.

The period from the mid-nineteenth century to 1911, when the National Insurance Act was passed, can be seen as the golden age of grassroots collectivism. Between 1908 and 1911, the government developed plans to turn the system into a statutory one. Participation was meant to become mandatory, and the state was to set the basic parameters for health insurance. We could see this as a first step from grassroots collectivism to state collectivism, and as the first clash between the two conceptions. *The Oddfellows Magazine* commented at the time (quoted in Green 1985: 111):

> Working men are awakening to the fact that this is a subtle attempt to take from the class to which they belong the administration of the great voluntary organizations which they have built up for themselves, and to hand over the future control to the paid servants of the governing class. [...] This is not liberty; this is not development of self-government, but a new form of autocracy and tyranny.

Another author in the same magazine argued (ibid.: 112):

To say, as the Bill now says, to the working class of the United Kingdom [...] 'you are unfit to be entrusted with the administration of your own money; [...] we will administer the money for you through committees' [...] [is] a flagrant insult to every working man and woman in the land. Why should working men and women be degraded to an inferior position?

But the Friendly Societies ultimately accepted the Act, and it turned out that their worst fears did not come to pass. They did lose some autonomy, and they also lost bargaining power vis-à-vis the medical professions. But the Friendly Societies found a place in the National Health Insurance (NHI) system, and self-governance remained a guiding principle of healthcare in the UK.

In 1946, however, members of the Friendly Societies, the trade unions and the voluntary hospitals realised that this time would be different. They realised that there was no hope of retaining autonomy under a fully nationalised system. When, in a desperate last attempt to save his plan, Bevan offered a series of concessions in 1948 – opt-outs and independence guarantees – it was already too late. By then, it had become clear to the opponents that while these guarantees might look good on paper, they would always remain mere promises that the government of the day would be able to erode, or revoke, at any time.

Bevan was not troubled by the conflict with the medical professions and the opposition parties. But resistance from the people whom he saw as the main beneficiaries of his reform plans affected him greatly. One of Bevan's most famous lines is 'How can wealth persuade poverty to use its political freedom to keep wealth in power? Here lies the whole art of Conservative politics in the twentieth century.' Bevan did not say that until several years later, and in a completely different context, but this quote – an echo of the Marxist theory of 'false consciousness' – nonetheless captures his attitude to those who opposed his healthcare nationalisation plans. In Bevan's view, his opponents simply failed to understand that nationalised healthcare was in their own best interest. He saw them as fooled by petit bourgeois notions of 'autonomy' and 'plurality'.

Bevan's behaviour in public became increasingly erratic. The government's popularity ratings sank, and his party began to see Bevan, their erstwhile rising star, as a burden. The plotting and backstabbing began. Bevan, already under external pressure, now came under internal pressure from within his own government and his own party as well.

When Bevan finally resigned in 1948, the idea of a state-run 'National Health Service' was dead in the water. No British politician ever touched it again.

But with Bevan's resignation, the hard work had only begun. Striking down a proposal was one thing, but the real challenge now was to come up with a better alternative. All stakeholders agreed that a return to the pre-war status quo ante was not an option. Bevan's successor, Ken Bowman, an economist who would later become a co-founder of the emerging science of health economics, came up with an entirely different leitmotiv for reform. He believed that the old system's main problems did not lie on the supply side, but on the demand side. The system generally worked well for the majority of people. It was not a complete coincidence that the UK had one of the highest life expectancies in the world (Roser 2016). But the problem was that the good quality healthcare, which the system could offer, was not open to everybody. There was wide variation on the basis of geography, income, occupation, and the financial situation of different health insurers.

Bowman addressed this problem in two steps. Firstly, a commission was set up to work out a minimum 'healthcare basket', a list of treatments that every insurer had to cover, and for which every household had to purchase insurance coverage. Secondly, he introduced two types of subsidies. The first was simply a means-tested premium subsidy, which would ensure that the basic health insurance package was affordable to everybody. The second was a subsidy for associations that disproportionately insured 'bad risks'. All insurers had to pay a fixed amount per policyholder into a common pool (the so-called 'risk structure compensation fund' or RSCF), and were refunded an amount that was adjusted for the health risk profile of the population they insured. In essence, this meant that if an association insured a lot of people in poor health, it would receive more from the RSCF than it paid into it, and if it insured a lot of people in good health, it would pay more into the RSCF than it received back. At least in theory, the RSCF created a level-playing field for all insurers, regardless of the health profile of their policyholders. In this way, it also created a level playing field between sick people and healthy people. An insurer would have no incentive to discriminate against a sick person, because once net transfers from/into the RSCF were taken into account, a sick person was just as attractive to the insurer as a healthy person.

Ultimately, of course, it was not the insurers who paid into the RSCF, but their clients. The RSCF system was a systematic redistribution from people in good health to people in poor health. The former paid higher premiums than they would have without the RSCF. This was, however, accepted without protest. People who enjoyed the good fortune of good health were, in the main, prepared to support those who were not so lucky. There was widespread support for the principle, expressed by Bevan, that '[i]llness is [not] an offence for which [people] should be penalised, but a misfortune, the cost of which should be shared by the community'. Bevan's plan had failed, but, although in a completely different way, this basic principle had now nonetheless become a reality.

Bowman's other main legacy is the principle of prefunding. Healthcare costs tend to rise systematically with age, and are heavily biased towards the end of life. Insurers were therefore required to accumulate old-age reserves on behalf of their members. This gave rise to old-age healthcare funds, which work, in principle, like pension funds, in that they are built up over the course of a person's working life, and used up over the course of their retirement. The only difference is that people do not directly access their old-age healthcare fund. Rather, their insurer uses it in order to pay for the higher healthcare costs associated with old age. This put healthcare funding on a more secure, sustainable footing.

For most people, little changed in practice, which is why the late 1940s and early 1950s are generally remembered as a period of a return to normal, as far as healthcare is concerned. Throughout the 1950s and 1960s, there was a remarkable degree of continuity. Most people chose their health insurer on the basis of occupation or place of residence, and switching rates were low, so families often remained with the same insurer for generations. The old Friendly Societies remained the dominant players in the insurance market.

In the more individualistic 1970s, such traditional group loyalties began to weaken. People began to see themselves as consumers as well as club members, and began to shop around for attractive alternatives. Slowly but surely, the insurance market became more competitive and dynamic. A series of mergers and acquisitions began, leading to a long period of market consolidation, although at the same time, the number of new market entrants also increased.

These changes in insurance markets had important ramifications for provider markets. Up until the 1970s, most insurers only held contracts with a small number of providers, and for hospitals and clinics that small number was often 'one'. 'Which hospital do you want to go to?' was not a question one would often hear at GP surgeries, except maybe in the sense of 'which of the two local ones'. In the 1970s, people began to demand greater levels of provider choice, and insurers had to respond. Some achieved this by simply contracting with a greater number of providers. Others made their reimbursement practices more flexible, so that patients would get their treatment costs reimbursed even if they sought treatment from a provider with whom their insurer did not have an explicit contract. Some sought in-between solutions, offering full reimbursement for contracted providers, and reimbursement with co-payments for non-contracted ones. Some offered completely unrestricted choice, allowing people to seek treatment from any registered medical provider in the country.

Increased demand for provider choice led to an increase in demand for information. People had always known that some hospitals and clinics were better than others, but up until the 1970s, there was not much hard evidence to back this up. From then on, medical outcomes data (especially standardised mortality rates), as well as more elaborate ratings, assessments and rankings, became more widely available. Hospitals and clinics with abnormally high standardised mortality rates would be hounded by the press, while those who had especially good results would shout about it from the rooftops. It came as a bit of a shock that differences in outcomes were much larger than expected, but this transparency shock ultimately proved helpful.

Insurers began to base their contracting decisions, among other things, on outcome data. Poorly performing providers would lose contracts and custom, well-performing ones would gain them. These changes in commissioning would shake up the provider landscape. Clinical guidelines were developed. Benchmarking and learning from best practice became much more deeply engrained in the sector. Modern management and quality control techniques, which had thus far bypassed the health sector, were being introduced.

These developments began slowly in the 1970s, and sped up massively in the 1980s. The decline in traditional heavy industries, and the related decline in trade union membership, weakened class-based and occupation-based social identities. Many of the old mutual insurance associations, built on a strong working-class identity, found it hard to adapt to this new environment. Some of them eventually worked out ways to combine their traditional solidaristic ethos with a professional business approach. But others saw their market share dwindle, some were forced to merge with others, and some disappeared altogether.

The 'Big Bang' of 1986 gave another big boost to competition, because it made old-age reserves portable between insurers. Previously, when people changed insurer, they would lose those funds, and their new insurer would have to build up old-age funds on their behalf from scratch. People above a certain age were therefore not attractive to insurers, and while they were not legally allowed to reject them, they did not actively woo them either. This changed when old-age funds were redefined as the policyholder's personal property, which they could transfer between insurers as often as they liked. Elderly people suddenly became attractive to insurers, because even though these people incurred higher medical expenses, they also brought an old-age fund with them, from which those expenses could be met.

As the country became more relaxed about the profit motive, for-profit insurers and for-profit providers experienced an unprecedented surge in their market shares. As the economy became more globalised, so did the health sector. Foreign companies started to take a keen interest in the British market. Today, 'Medi-Partenaires', 'Tokushukai', 'Kaiser Permanente', 'Asklepios-Kliniken' and others are household names, but back in the early 1980s, they were exotic newcomers. Established providers resented them, and asked the government to protect them from 'unfair' competition. But these newcomers brought new business models, new technologies and new medical know-how with them.

Insurers also began to offer a greater variety of healthcare plans. While they had previously only offered one standard contract, they now began to offer plans with deductibles, coupled with a personal Medical Savings Account, in return for premium discounts. Plans which offered perks, such as single room accommodation in hospitals, at a surcharge, also became available. Integrated provider networks, with clearly established clinical pathways, also sprang up, competing with the traditional stand-alone medical facility.

This period also brought greater variation in the extent, type and depth of vertical integration. This is a feature of our health system which often confuses foreign visitors. A lot of countries have a complete insurer–provider split, meaning that health insurance and healthcare provision are completely separate activities, not unlike car insurance and car repair services. In other countries, this split does not exist: the two functions are integrated. Such systems work more like a gym chain, where members are entitled to use the facilities in return for a monthly fee, but where we would not think of the revenue collection and the financing as separate from the actual running of the gym. In the UK, both the 'gym model' and the 'car insurance model' exist – and so does virtually everything in between. Some insurers run healthcare facilities of their own, and employ their own clinical staff. This can range from a handful of basic primary care facilities and/or pharmacies to a full network of multi-speciality clinics. Others do not directly own anything, but maintain close contractual ties with networks of preferred providers, and try to shape the delivery of healthcare in this way. Similar variation exists in terms of horizontal integration.

This means that there is not really such a thing as 'the healthcare system', but a great variety of different models of organising healthcare. To British people, the question: 'How does healthcare work in your country?' makes no more sense than the question 'How does leisure work in your country?' The answer, in both cases, is that there is no answer. Different people do different things, and different service providers are organised in different ways. This is true in what we could loosely call 'the leisure industry', and it is true in healthcare. The question would, of course, make perfect sense if healthcare were organised, or even run, by the state. But then, if leisure were organised, or even run, by the state, the question 'How does leisure work in your country?' would also make perfect sense.

More recently, social and demographic changes have left their mark on the health sector. In the larger towns and cities, healthcare groups catering to immigrant communities have sprung up, with Polish-, Punjabi- and Urdu-speaking groups being especially prominent. Patient associations, representing people with specific conditions, have taken on a more proactive role in negotiating group contracts and commissioning healthcare services for their target populations.

In short, the system has gone through its fair share of changes since the post-war days. Each change has triggered a tendency to romanticise the old ways in retrospect, even if, overall, it can hardly be denied that the system has grown much more sophisticated and consumer-focused over time. Public appreciation of the system has had its ups and downs, and there have always been periodic outbreaks of popular healthcare-industry-bashing. Is the discontent we currently witness just one of those outbreaks? Or is there more to it this time?

We can draw an analogy with another sector that suffers from a bad press: air travel. If you judged that sector by the way it is represented in popular culture, or in watercooler conversations, you would think that there has never been a worse time to get on an airplane. Delayed flights, cancelled flights, dodgy pricing policies with hidden fees, ludicrous excess baggage charges, lost luggage, poor or non-existent customer service, overcrowded airports, inconveniently located airports with poor transport links, terrible food, annoying advertisements on board – you get the drift. But at the same time, fares have been falling steeply in real terms, while the number of destinations has multiplied, and the sector has been expanding at phenomenal rates. A former luxury good has become a mass market product. But while the sector has improved, our expectations have adjusted upwards, and while we quickly forget an experience which meets our expectations, we do not so easily forget one which does not. Perhaps more importantly, because of our intuitive dislike of the profit motive, we are quick to suspect bad faith. We let the perfect be the enemy of the good, whether it is on the plane or in hospital. However, our healthcare system's international reputation is infinitely better than its domestic one. Health economists and health policy advisers from all over the developed world, and beyond, continue to flock to Britain to study our system. Countless health reforms abroad have been modelled on the British example, including Switzerland's acclaimed *Krankenversicherungsgesetz* from 1996, and the successful Dutch *Zorgverzekeringswet* from 2006. In 1990, instead of simply adopting the West German system as part of a reunification 'package deal', East Germany deliberately went for something much closer to the British system. Together with higher education, healthcare continues to be one of our major exports, with foreign patients bringing in almost as much revenue as foreign students. Health insurers in neighbouring countries have long maintained contracts with British clinics, and in the last decade, the growing middle classes of China, India and other emerging economies have begun to flock here in large numbers. And while other countries struggle with the financial pressures associated with falling birth rates and increased longevity, our health insurers have accumulated old-age reserves worth over £900 billion.

If Bevan were alive today, would he find much to like in our healthcare system? Probably not. But even he would, grudgingly, have to concede that his central goals have been achieved, even if not in the way he intended.

Back to reality

This description of events after the spring of 1946 is entirely fictional – and yet, it is not as absurd and far-fetched as it will probably seem to the reader. For a start, the popular folk memory of how the NHS was founded has been heavily mythologised in retrospect. According to the popular narrative, the NHS was created in response to pressure from below – a victory of ordinary people getting together, organising collectively, and fighting for their rights. The NHS, in this version of events, is one of the finest expressions of 'People Power'.

This is the story told by, for example, RAF veteran Harry Leslie Smith, who, in 2014, became a minor political celebrity for retelling it:

> [The time before the NHS] was an uncivilised time because public healthcare didn't exist. Back then, hospitals, doctors and medicine were for the privileged few. Because they were run by profit rather than for vital state service that keeps a nation, its citizens and workers, fit and healthy. [...] Sadly, rampant poverty, and no healthcare, were the norm for the Britain of my youth. That injustice galvanised my generation, to become, after the Second World War, the tide that raised all boats. [...] Election Day 1945 was one of the proudest days of my life. I felt that I was finally getting a chance to grab destiny by the shirt collar. And that is why I voted [...] for the creation of the NHS.[3]

Columnist Owen Jones tells the same story, but wraps it into his broader ordinary-people-vs-elites narrative:

> The welfare state, the NHS, workers' rights: these were the culmination of generations of struggle, not least by a labour movement that had set up the Labour party – controversially at the time – to give working people a voice.[4]

---

3 Speech by Harry Leslie Smith at the Labour Party Conference, 24 September 2014 (https://www.youtube.com/watch?v=E0FIFsgxJV4). See also Hunger, filth, fear and death: remembering life before the NHS. *New Statesman*, 31 October 2014.

4 Sorry, David Cameron, but your British history is not mine. *The Guardian*, 15 June 2014.

The same story is all over Ken Loach's genre classic 'The Spirit of '45'; it is retold in Michael Moore's interview with Tony Benn in the documentary 'Sicko', and there were traces of it in the opening ceremony of the London Olympics as well.

It is a powerful story that continues to arouse strong feelings. But it is not a true story. The creation of the NHS had little to do with pressure from below; it was not a change that ordinary people had fought for. Far from being People Power in action, the NHS was a brainchild of social elites, to which the general public just passively acquiesced. The idea that the organised working classes were demanding a government takeover of healthcare is a post-hoc rationalisation, which projects the fondness for the NHS, which the public *subsequently* developed, back into the period of its creation.

In a paper in the *English Historical Review*, Nick Hayes (2012: 659) analyses a wide range of healthcare-related opinion surveys from the 1930s and 1940s. He concludes:

> [T]he evidence before us seems to indicate a fairly large amount of resistance to State interference in the field of medicine [...] roughly half the population was opposed to any major change on the health front, a quarter disinterested and a quarter in favour of State intervention.

Similarly, in an analysis of the political factors which drove the creation of publicly funded healthcare programmes in the UK and North America, Hacker (1998: 63) finds:

> [F]ew of the scholars who have addressed this period have attempted to show that the passage of compulsory health insurance [...] was a response to widespread popular pressure. In fact, this would be difficult to do, since the overwhelming evidence is that these early programs were promulgated by government elites well in advance of public demands.

Nor was the pre-NHS system as bleak as commonly imagined. The UK had a well-developed healthcare system before 1948, and indeed before 1911, a system which had deep roots in the working-class mutualism of the nineteenth century (Green 1985). What happened in 1948 was not the creation of a new system, but a government takeover of an existing one.

There were substantial improvements in health after the creation of the NHS. But there were also substantial improvements in health *before* the creation of the NHS. In long-term time series of population health data, the impact of the introduction of the NHS is not even discernible. Pre-NHS trends and patterns – positive and negative ones – mostly continued. Median life expectancy, for example, had already been increasing steadily since the 1860s, from around 45 years back then to over 70 years at around the time the NHS was founded (ONS 2012a).[5] From then on, the rate of increase actually slowed down, because the major advances against infectious diseases had already been made (ONS 2012b: 2).

Even among the poor, the creation of the NHS did not change trends in aggregate health outcomes. Gregory (2009) analyses the link between poverty and health outcomes in both the early 1900s and early 2000s. He finds that while there have been huge improvements in health across the board, there has been no narrowing of the 'health gap' (ibid.: 6):

> [T]he link between mortality and deprivation across England and Wales remains as strong today as it was a century ago. [...] [T]here is no evidence that [...] the relation between mortality and deprivation has lessened to any significant degree.

The pre-NHS system had major faults, the most serious being its coverage gaps, which meant that some people fell through the

---

5 The trend for average life expectancy is about the same, but median life expectancy is arguably a more relevant measure. In earlier centuries, levels of infant mortality were so high that they completely dominate average life expectancy figures.

cracks. This is why the post-war emphasis on universality was absolutely appropriate. But this aim could have been achieved within the existing system, or, indeed, in *any* alternative system. Health systems in the developed world differ in lots of respects, but in one way or another, virtually all of them – the US being the only major outlier – have achieved universal access to a broad package of healthcare services (see OECD 2012). So have, for that matter, plenty of middle-income countries. The UK is by no means the only country where access to healthcare does not depend on a person's ability to pay, but it is probably the only developed country where this is still celebrated as if it were an outstanding achievement. We cannot know what the alternative would have been if the NHS had never been created. But whatever it would have been, it is safe to say that Britain would soon have found some way to close the remaining coverage gaps.

It also seems safe to say that if Bevan's plan had failed (and its success was by no means guaranteed), the NHS would not have been created at a later stage, and we would certainly not create it today. The well-worn cliché about the NHS being 'the envy of the world' raises the question why 'the world' refuses to move closer to the system it supposedly envies. Most of the developed world has gone for mixed private–public systems, with some combination of political direction and market forces. In countries which have not created national health services, even socialist and communist parties are not calling for their creation today.[6] And there is a good reason for that: it is simply not a particularly successful model.

---

6 A good example would be Germany's Die Linke, the legal heir of the Socialist Unity Party (SED), which was the governing party of the former GDR. Among other things, Die Linke (2011: 42–45) calls for the abolition of co-payments, for a more progressive financing of health insurance costs, for price controls on pharmaceuticals, for a near abolition of for-profit health insurance, and for restrictions on how financial surpluses can be used. If these demands were realised, it would create a heavily regulated, highly politicised health sector. But it would still stop well short of the creation of a national health service.

Chapter 2 of this monograph will provide a comparative evaluation of different health systems in terms of health outcomes, quality, efficiency and sustainability, with a particular focus on the much overhyped Commonwealth Fund study. It will show that despite some commendable improvements since the early 2000s, the NHS remains an international laggard on most available measures. While the NHS's achievements are mostly a matter of mythology, its failures are very real.

On the positive side, though, the NHS is not the reform-resistant monolith it may sometimes appear to be. Chapter 3 will document some of the most important health reforms that have taken place in the UK over the past quarter century. It will show that, despite many detours and wrong turns, the NHS has broadly changed in the right direction, especially with its cautious introduction of 'quasi-market' mechanisms. This reform course has stalled, but it could, and should, be resumed and revitalised.

While speculative, the 'alternative history' above is not entirely plucked out of thin air. It contains some allusions to how healthcare really did evolve in countries that chose to secure universal access within a broadly market-based settlement. Chapter 4 will describe a few of those systems, namely the Swiss, the Dutch, the German, the Belgian and the Israeli systems. These have their fair share of problems as well, especially when it comes to managing healthcare cost inflation, but they are still considerably superior to the NHS on a wide range of outcome measures.

The alternative history above is, of course, not just speculation about what *might* have happened. It describes an alternative which would, in the author's view, have been desirable, or at least preferable to what actually happened. There used to be a saying in the former Eastern bloc countries that one can easily turn an aquarium into a fish soup, but that one cannot so easily turn a fish soup back into an aquarium. This applies to healthcare systems as well. The old Friendly Societies, the voluntary hospitals, the trade union–linked mutual insurance schemes and all the other independent actors of the pre-1948 health system have gone. Nonetheless, Chapter 5 will outline a rough fish-soup-into-aquarium conversion plan. It will present a roadmap for moving from where we are today to a pluralistic system, with a particular emphasis on keeping disruption to a minimum. Chapter 5 is not a blueprint for a revolution. It just presents a few pragmatic steps which would not change much on their own, but which would set the health system on a completely different long-term path.

This leaves the obvious question whether fundamental health reform, even if technically possible, will ever be politically feasible in the UK, given the status of the NHS as a 'national religion'. Many supporters of a free economy have effectively written off health reform in the UK as a lost cause (e.g. Lal 2012; Hannan 2015). The public, they argue, reveres the NHS too much to even contemplate alternative arrangements. The emotional attachment to the health service is so strong, and runs so deep, that arguments for a pluralistic system will never be given a fair hearing. Indeed, to those of us who regularly make the case for such a system, it can sometimes seem like that. This is especially so when arguments for system-level changes are misrepresented as a denigration of individual doctors and nurses; when references to the Swiss or the Dutch system are misrepresented as a call for the introduction of the American system; or when arguments about the ownership of healthcare facilities are misrepresented as a call for denying treatment to poor people.

But it is important to distinguish between the aggressive 'NHS purism' which dominates the public debate, and which is indeed not responsive to reasoned argument, and the views of the wider public. There is a vocal minority of purists who denounce every minor tweak in health policy as an assault on the NHS, and indeed on the very notion of universal healthcare. This tendency is expressed in news headlines and book titles such as those listed in Box 1, giving the healthcare debate a hysterical and paranoid tone.

Box 1 A selection of titles

Media

'Why privatisation is killing the NHS' (*Huffington Post*, 23 September 2014), 'The NHS is on the brink of extinction – we need to shout about it' (*The Guardian*, 8 January 2014), 'The NHS privatisation experiment is unravelling before our eyes' (*New Statesman*, 9 January 2015), 'Farewell to the NHS, 1948–2013: a dear and trusted friend finally murdered by Tory ideologues' (*Independent*, 31 March 2013), 'NHS "Jarrow March": Hundreds protest against "privatisation"' (BBC News, 16 August 2014), 'NHS sell-out: Tories sign largest privatisation deal in history worth £780MILLION' (*Daily Mirror*, 12 March 2015), 'TTIP could make NHS privatisation "irreversible", warns Unite union' (*Huffington Post*, 3 July 2014) and 'Privatisation is ripping the NHS from our hands' (*The Guardian*, 6 August 2014).

Books

The End of the NHS (Pollock [forthcoming]), *NHS for Sale: Myths, Lies and Deception* (Davis et al. 2015), *How to Dismantle the NHS in 10 Easy Steps* (El-Gingihy 2015), *NHS SOS: How the NHS Was Betrayed – And How We Can Save It* (Davis and Tallis 2013), *The Plot Against the NHS* (Player and Leys 2011), *Betraying the NHS: Health Abandoned* (Mandelstam 2007) and *NHS Plc: The Privatisation of Our Health Care* (Pollock 2004).

The idea that there is a 'secret agenda' to dismantle the NHS, and replace it with a copy of the American system, has been around for decades (Niemietz 2015c). It lacks a factual basis, but it does give rise to a no-smoke-without-fire effect ('It may be exaggerated, but surely, they would not all say that without reason').

However, public opinion on healthcare is more multidimensional than the media coverage and the political debate around the subject suggest. The British Social Attitudes Survey reveals an interesting contrast. When people are asked about their commitment to the NHS in the abstract, support is indeed near-unanimous and strongly felt (Gershlick et al. 2015). This is in line with previous findings (Taylor 2013: 7–8). But on the other hand, when people are asked about whether they would personally prefer to be treated by an NHS provider, a private for-profit or a private non-profit provider, 43 per cent indicate no general preference for either sector. A further 18 per cent express an active preference for independent sector providers. This is a remarkable result given that 'social desirability bias' (the phenomenon of people giving the answer they think they are socially expected to give, rather than disclosing their true views) surely works against these options. Among people born after 1979, only about a third have a general preference for NHS providers.

What enjoys near-unanimous support in the UK is the principle of universality: people want a cast-iron guarantee that access to high-quality healthcare will never be determined by individual ability to pay. Apart from that, the majority of people seem to be quite pragmatic about the organisational details of the health system. The core principles are non-negotiable; everything else is open for debate. This monograph is written in precisely that spirit.

2 WHO SHOULD ENVY WHOM? NHS PERFORMANCE FROM AN INTERNATIONAL PERSPECTIVE[1]

'NHS: UK now has one of the worst healthcare systems in the developed world, according to OECD report', read a headline in the *Independent* newspaper in November 2015.[2] The article summarised the report as follows: 'the quality of care in the UK is "poor to mediocre" across several key health areas [...] and the NHS struggles to get even the "basics" right [...] Britain was placed on a par with Chile and Poland'. Referring to the same report, the *Financial Times* wrote: 'Britons are less likely to survive a heart attack, stroke and leading cancers than people in many other developed nations, according to an assessment of international health systems'.[3]

Such reports will have come as a surprise to many readers. Just one and a half years earlier, the Commonwealth Fund's international ranking of healthcare systems had put the NHS at no. 1 (Davis et al. 2014). This had been widely reported in the British media as 'proof' that the NHS was indeed the best healthcare system in the world.[4] So how can the developed world's best healthcare system almost simultaneously be one of its worst?

---

1 This chapter is based on Niemietz (2016).

2 http://www.independent.co.uk/life-style/health-and-families/health-news/nhs
-uk-now-has-one-of-the-worst-healthcare-systems-in-the-developed-world-accord
ing-to-oecd-report-a6721401.html

3 http://www.ft.com/cms/s/0/8d3cc7e8-8267-11e5-a01c-8650859a4767.html#axzz
3yAZeI1Nb

4 See, for example: NHS comes top in healthcare survey, *The Guardian*, 17 June 2014;
NHS means British healthcare rated top out of 11 western countries, with US

This chapter will give an overview of how the NHS is performing in terms of health outcomes, quality and efficiency. This should not be confused with an account of population health: the health status of the population is affected by myriad factors which have little or nothing to do with healthcare. Socioeconomic factors, demographics, dietary habits, alcohol and tobacco consumption, physical activity, environmental quality and genetics may well explain a greater share of the international variation in health outcomes than health systems.

This chapter, then, is only concerned with those health outcomes that are predominantly attributable to the health system. Age-adjusted survival rates for prominent conditions are the most conventional type of measure. If Country A has a greater proportion of people dying from, for example, lung cancer than Country B, we would not draw conclusions about these countries' health systems. It probably tells us more about differences in the prevalence and intensity of smoking (past and present), in air pollution, exposure to chemicals, genetic predisposition and other risk factors than it tells us about healthcare. However, once people *have* developed lung cancer, their chances of surviving the next five years depend critically on the quality and timeliness of the healthcare they receive. Survival rates are therefore a fair way of assessing health systems.

Cancer

In high-income countries, cancers are among the leading causes of death, not least because medically less challenging conditions have been successfully conquered. There are over 100 different types of cancer, but the five most common ones, taken together, account for 56 per cent of all cancer cases diagnosed in the UK

---

coming last, *The Independent*, 17 June 2014; Britain's NHS is the world's best healthcare system, says report, *Daily Telegraph*, 17 June 2014.

Figure 1   Age-adjusted breast cancer 5-year relative survival rates,
diagnosed in 2008 or latest available year

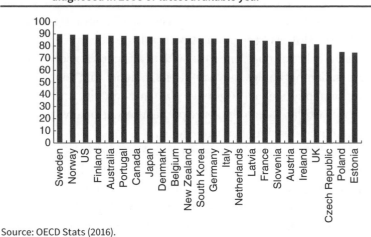

Source: OECD Stats (2016).

every year (based on Cancer Research UK 2015). Figures 1–5
show age-adjusted five-year survival rates for these five cancers.[5]

The most common type of cancer in the UK is breast cancer,
with about 53,700 new cases diagnosed each year (ibid.). The UK's
five-year survival rate for breast cancer is 81.1 per cent, the lowest rate among high-income countries in this sample. This rate is
about five percentage points below South Korea's, the 12th-best
performer on this measure, and a difference of five percentage
points in survival rates translates into over 2,500 excess deaths
per year. So we might say that if the UK's breast cancer patients

5   'Age-adjusted' means relative to a randomly selected group with the same age
composition in the same country. This corrects for the fact that if the average
age of cancer patients is, for example, 50 in Country 1, and 75 in Country 2, then
of course Country 1 will have a higher overall survival rate, even if the under-
lying quality of medical care is identical. 'Age-adjustment' means simulating a
situation in which all countries' patient populations had the same age profile.
In the figures, I have excluded countries where the confidence interval around the
survival rates is larger than five percentage points, because this means that data for
these countries are too erratic to draw meaningful conclusions. This leads to the
exclusion of a handful of small countries such as Iceland.

Figure 2   Age-adjusted prostate cancer 5-year relative survival rates, diagnosed 2005–9

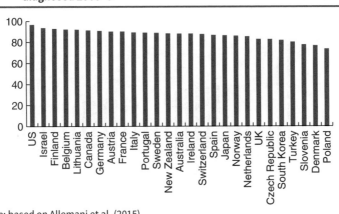

Source: based on Allemani et al. (2015).

were treated in South Korea rather than on the NHS, an extra 2,500 lives could be extended every year (see Figure 1).

Prostate cancer is the second most common type of cancer in the UK, with just over 47,000 new cases per year (ibid.). The UK's five-year survival rate of 83.2 per cent is lower than in most other developed countries. For patients in Sweden, which ranks 12th, the chance of survival is six percentage points higher, which means that if British patients had been treated in Sweden, an extra 2,800 might have lived beyond the five-year period (see Figure 2).

Prostate cancer is closely followed by lung cancer in terms of prevalence, with about 45,500 new cases detected every year (ibid.). At less than 10 per cent, the UK has, again, the lowest survival rate of all high-income countries in this sample, with plenty of upper/middle-income countries achieving better results. Survival rates are over five percentage points higher in Australia, which ranks 12th on this count. This is equivalent to over 2,400 lives which might have been lengthened if the UK's lung cancer patients had been treated by the Australian system rather than on the NHS (see Figure 3).

Figure 3 Age-adjusted lung cancer 5-year relative survival rates, diagnosed 2005–9

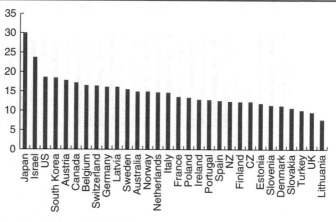

Source: based on Allemani et al. (2015).

Figure 4 Age-adjusted bowel cancer 5-year relative survival rates, diagnosed 2008 or latest available year

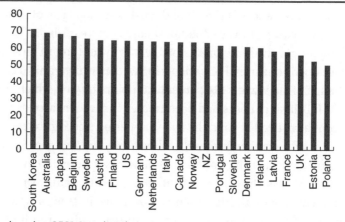

Source: based on OECD Stats (2016).

The fourth most common type of cancer in the UK is bowel cancer, with over 41,000 new cases detected each year (ibid.). The UK has, once again, the lowest five-year survival rate of all

Figure 5 Age-adjusted melanoma 5-year relative survival rates, diagnosed 2000–7

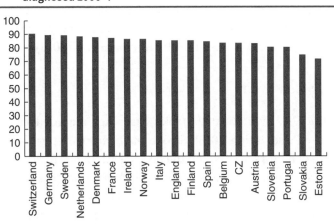

Source: based on Eurocare (2014).

high-income countries in the sample, trailing more than seven percentage points behind Canada, the 12th best. The annual number of excess deaths, when choosing Canada as a benchmark, is over 3,000 (see Figure 4).

Finally, melanoma, a form of skin cancer, is diagnosed about 14,500 times per year, which makes it the fifth most common form of cancer in the UK (ibid.). For melanoma survival rates, I have only found data from Eurocare, which is naturally limited to European countries. In this smaller country sample, England occupies a middling position (see Figure 5).

As mentioned, there are over 100 types of cancer, and all developed countries do well on some of them and badly on others. But the five types of cancer discussed above are by far the most common ones, and taken together, they account for the majority of all cancer diagnoses. So a country's performance on these five measures can be seen as a good proxy for its performance on cancer care overall.

It is worth pointing out, however, that while the UK results look sobering in a snapshot perspective, the time trend is a much more positive one. In the late 1990s and early 2000s, the NHS used to trail much further behind comparable countries than it currently does, reflecting significant catch-up growth in the meantime (see OECD Stats 2016; Allemani et al. 2015).

Stroke

In the UK, over 150,000 stroke cases are recorded each year (Stroke Association 2016). Stroke *incidence* is determined by a range of factors over which the health system has little or no control, but again a patient's chances of *surviving* a stroke have a lot to do with the quality and timeliness of healthcare.

Strokes come in different varieties. Ischaemic strokes are by far the most common, accounting for more than four out of five cases (ibid.). Figure 6 shows age-standardised and sex-standardised 30-day mortality rates for stroke patients. In the UK, the rate is 9.2 per cent, 2.3 percentage points higher than the rate achieved by the 12th-best performer, Switzerland. The difference

Figure 6   Ischaemic stroke 30-day mortality rates (age/sex-standardised), 2014 or latest available year

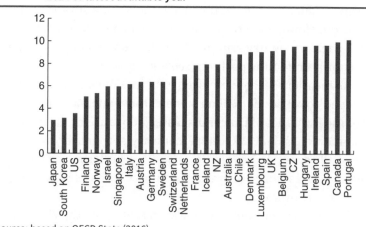

Source: based on OECD Stats (2016).

Figure 7   Haemorrhagic stroke 30-day mortality rate (age/sex-standardised), 2014 or latest available year

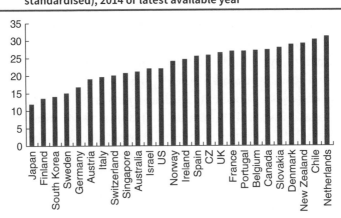

Source: based on OECD Stats (2016).

may seem small, but it still amounts to around 3,000 lives that could be saved if NHS care rose to Swiss standards.

Haemorrhagic strokes account for a much smaller proportion of strokes. The British mortality rate, at 26.5 per cent, is more than four percentage points higher than the rate of the US and Israel, which share a joint 12th place. This difference translates into over 1,000 excess deaths (see Figure 7).

Again, it needs pointing out that what may not look impressive in a snapshot perspective hides a fairly impressive trend of catching up over time (Appleby 2011). The NHS lags behind other countries, but not nearly as much as it used to.

Amenable mortality

Amenable mortality (AM), also known as 'mortality amenable to healthcare', is a more holistic measure of health system performance. It compares a country's actual mortality profile to the hypothetical profile we would observe under an 'optimal' health system, in which every life that could, in theory, be saved through medical treatment really is being saved (Gay et al. 2011). AM compares the actual to the ideal.

AM still has some major flaws, not least the fact that 'amenable to healthcare' does not necessarily mean 'attributable to the health system'. AM figures strip out causes of death that are completely beyond the health system's reach, such as incurable diseases or accidents leading to instant death. But unlike survival rates, AM figures are not adjusted for differences in the overall incidence of different conditions, and the latter is determined by factors over which the health system has very little control. In other words, AM figures still fail to control for some of the most important non-healthcare factors influencing health outcomes.

Still, AM figures tell us a lot more about the performance of different health systems than unadjusted mortality figures. Unfortunately, recent figures are only available for European countries. Figure 8 shows the number of deaths per 100,000 people that could have been avoided through better and/or timelier

Figure 8   Amenable mortality: standardised death rates per 100,000 inhabitants, 2012 or latest available year

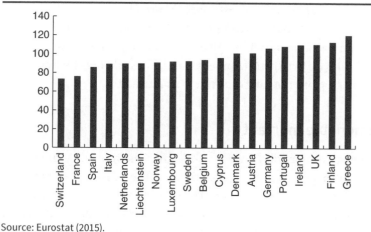

Source: Eurostat (2015).

healthcare. Unsurprisingly, no country comes close to zero: there are avoidable deaths in every health system, because no system achieves excellence across the board.

Among Western European countries, AM is lowest in Switzerland, France, Spain, Italy and the Netherlands. It is highest in Greece, Finland, the UK, Ireland and Portugal. There are about 111 avoidable deaths per 100,000 people in the UK every year. If that figure could be reduced to the rate observed in Denmark, about 5,600 lives would be saved each year.

It is, however, also worth noting that the NHS has been showing greater improvement than most other systems over time (Gay et al. 2011). As before, while the snapshot perspective is sobering, the time series data are far more encouraging.

Waiting times

Internationally comparable data on waiting times are only available for a handful of countries (Siciliani et al. 2014). The waiting time indicators contained in the Euro Health Consumer Index (EHCI) (Björnberg 2015) have to be the nearest substitute, but they cannot tell us how long people actually wait for treatment. They are based on patient associations' assessment of how likely it is that a representative patient will wait for longer than a specified reference period. Countries are then given scores on this basis, with a green score meaning fast access, a red score meaning long waits, and a yellow score being somewhere in between.

EHCI scores therefore give too much weight to arbitrary cut-off points, and responses may also be skewed by factors such as 'availability bias'. And yet, they are the closest thing we have to data on waiting times.

Table 1 presents results for GP appointments and A&E visits. England, together with Sweden and Lithuania, scores red on both counts, meaning that A&E waiting times normally exceed

Table 1   Waiting times for GP appointments and at A&E
           departments, 2014

| | GP | | |
A&E	Green (= same-day appointment is the norm)	Yellow	Red (= same-day appointment usually not possible)
Green (<1 hour)	Belgium Denmark Netherlands Portugal Switzerland Czech Republic Hungary	Norway	Finland Iceland
Yellow	Austria Latvia Luxembourg Slovakia	Germany Slovenia	Estonia Greece Poland Spain
Red (>3 hours)	France Italy Malta	Ireland	Lithuania Sweden England

Source: based on Björnberg (2015).

three hours, and that securing a same-day appointment with a
GP is difficult.

Table 2 is about waiting times for major surgeries (coronary
bypass, coronary angioplasty, hip replacement, knee joint replacement) and for the commencement of cancer therapy (radi-
ation and/or chemotherapy). England, together with Italy and
Hungary, scores yellow on both counts, meaning that most, but
by no means all, patients can expect cancer therapy to com-
mence within three weeks, and their surgery to be performed
within three months.

Finally, Table 3 shows access to specialists and waiting times
for CT scans, with the latter serving as a proxy for major diagnostics. For the former, the EHCI does not look at waiting times
as such, but at whether patients can book an appointment with a
specialist directly, without requiring a GP referral. This is prob-
lematic because *direct* access does not automatically mean *fast*
access.

Table 2   Waiting times for surgery and cancer therapy, 2014

Cancer therapy commencement	Major elective surgery		
	Green (>90 per cent within 3 months)	Yellow	Red (<50 per cent within 3 months)
Green (>90 per cent within 3 weeks)	Belgium Denmark Finland France Germany Luxembourg Switzerland	Austria Estonia	Iceland Malta Portugal Slovakia
Yellow	Netherlands	Hungary Italy England	Latvia Spain
Red (<50 per cent within 3 weeks)		Czech Republic Greece Lithuania Norway Sweden	Ireland Poland Slovenia

Source: based on Björnberg (2015).

England, together with Ireland, Malta, Spain and Sweden, scores red in both categories, meaning that in these countries patients will typically wait longer than three weeks for a CT scan, and there is a strict gatekeeping system in place.

Taken together, the English NHS receives four red scores, and not a single green one, whereas Switzerland, the Netherlands, Belgium, Luxembourg, Austria, Denmark and Finland receive at least four green scores. Despite the EHCI data's shortcomings, it is therefore fair to say that British patients face greater access barriers than patients in most comparable countries. Swift access to care is not one of the NHS's strengths.

Once again, though, it is worth pointing out that what may look unimpressive in a snapshot perspective looks very different in a time series perspective. Since the early 2000s, the NHS has made rapid progress in cutting waiting times across a range of services (Crisp 2011: 55–57). Today's waiting times may look

Table 3   Access to specialist care and waiting time for diagnostics

	Specialist access		
CT scan	*Green (unrestricted direct access)*	*Yellow (partial gate-keeping)*	*Red (gate-keeping)*
Green (<1 week)	Austria Belgium Switzerland	Czech Republic	Finland Netherlands
Yellow	Germany Greece Iceland Slovakia	Denmark Estonia France	Lithuania Norway Portugal
Red (>3 weeks)	Latvia Luxembourg	Hungary Italy Poland Slovenia	Ireland Malta Spain Sweden England

Source: based on Björnberg (2015).

excessive to, say, a Swiss expatriate living in the UK, but they will look very different to somebody who experienced typical waiting times in the 1990s.

The Commonwealth Fund study

Defenders of the current system tend to dismiss international comparisons as biased, flawed and meaningless, but there is one study which is exempt from their objections: the Commonwealth Fund study (Davis et al. 2014). The CF study – widely reported as the proof that the NHS is indeed the world's best healthcare system – has acquired something of a 'trump card' status in the British healthcare debate. As commentator Owen Jones put it: 'read the Commonwealth Fund report and weep into your Milton Friedman textbook'.[6]

---

6   A £10 charge to visit a GP would be just the start of a slippery slope for the NHS. *The Guardian*, 18 June 2014.

But the report does not actually show what Jones and many others seem to think it shows.

The 'healthy lives' category

The CF study is not primarily, or even secondarily, a study of health outcomes. Only one of its categories relates to outcomes, and if we look at that category in isolation, we find a familiar pattern: France, Sweden, Switzerland, Australia and the Netherlands make up the top five, and the UK comes out second to last (Table 4).

So it is not that the Commonwealth Fund comes to different conclusions from other studies: it just measures different things. But insofar as it does measure the same thing as other sources, it broadly comes to the same conclusions. This was inadvertently captured in *The Guardian*'s coverage of the report: 'The only serious black mark against the NHS was its poor record on keeping people alive'.

Table 4 The CF's ranking for health outcomes (the 'healthy lives' category), 2014

Rank	
1	France
2	Sweden
3	Switzerland
4	Australia
5	Netherlands
6	Norway
7	Germany
8	Canada
9	New Zealand
10	UK
11	US

There is no aggregate absolute score for this category in the report, which is why only the rank is shown.
Source: Davis et al. (2014)

The 'safe care' and 'efficiency' (sub)categories

Most categories in the CF studies are not about outcomes, but about inputs, procedures and general system features. There is something to be said for that approach. Studies that rely heavily on outcomes can identify differences in performance, but they cannot tell us much about what causes these differences. Most studies treat the health system as a black box that somehow turns inputs into outcomes, whereas the CF study tries to pry open the black box, and shed some light on what is going on inside.

This is ambitious, and it means that the study sometimes has to rely on strong, untested assumptions. The CF uses a specific protocol of how healthcare ought to be delivered, and judges health systems by the extent to which they comply with it. Deviations count as indications of poor healthcare. For example, two criteria by which the CF study evaluates safety is whether a doctor routinely receives a computerised alert or prompt about a potential problem with drug dose or interaction, and whether he or she routinely receives reminders for guideline-based interventions and/or tests (Davis et al. 2014: 15).

On these measures, the NHS performs very well, while the Norwegian and the Swiss systems perform poorly. This *may* indicate that the latter two systems offer low standards of drug safety. But this is speculation. They may also simply handle drug safety issues in other ways, or at a different level.

Similarly, one of the CF's measures of efficiency is the cost of administration as a share of total healthcare spending. This makes intuitive sense, but cutting back on administration does not automatically make a health system more efficient. The NHS could very easily slash administrative costs by simply moving back to the old system of block grants, under which providers were assigned lump sum budgets only loosely related to clinical need or activity levels. But this would almost certainly make the system as a whole less efficient, because it would lead to a misallocation of resources, and set poor incentives.

The 'access' and 'equity' categories

The study also contains criteria which systematically favour fully tax-funded single-payer systems. This is particularly true of the 'access' category, and to a lesser extent, the related 'equity' category.

For example, the CF asks patients whether their insurer has ever (fully or partially) declined a payment. Unsurprisingly, Sweden, Norway and the UK do best on this criterion – as they would, by definition, because these are not insurance-based systems, so there simply are no insurers that could decline payments. The CF also asks patients whether they have ever forgone medical care on cost grounds, or whether they have incurred cumulative out-of-pocket payments in excess of $1,000 over the past year. On the NHS, it would be virtually impossible to accumulate out-of-pocket payments anywhere near $1,000, so the UK receives top marks on this count. However, this does not mean that British patients enjoy unlimited access to expensive treatments. *All* health systems limit access to healthcare in one way or another; some rely more on user payments, others rely more on subtler forms of rationing. Ideally, a study on accessibility and equity should be neutral with regard to *how* different systems limit access, yet the CF study is anything but neutral. It registers pecuniary barriers – the relevant subcategory is called 'Cost-Related Access Problems' – but it is blind to rationing decisions taken behind the scenes (for example, through NICE[7] decisions). There are no subcategories called 'Non-Cost-Related Access Problems' or 'Rationing-Related Access Problems'.[8]

This strongly favours NHS-style systems by design. Suppose a new, expensive drug is available in Switzerland with a co-payment, while on the NHS it is not available at all, or very strictly rationed. The CF study would then register 'cost-related access problems' in Switzerland, but none whatsoever in the UK.

This is not just a hypothetical example. Richards (2010) documents cross-country variation in the consumption of various

---

7   National Institute for Health and Care Excellence, which appraises therapies in the UK.

8   There is a subcategory about waiting times, which is commendable, but it does not fully solve the problem. Long waiting times are just one rationing tool among many. If a treatment is simply not provided at all, the recorded waiting time is zero.

Figure 9   Drug consumption in the UK relative to a 14-country average

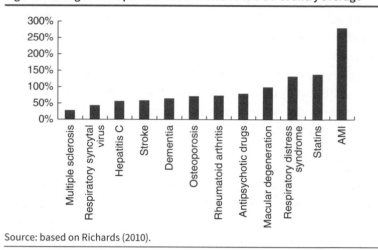

Source: based on Richards (2010).

innovative medicines, adjusted for differences in clinical need. UK consumption, relative to the average of the other countries in the sample (Australia, Austria, Canada, Denmark, France, Germany, Italy, New Zealand, Norway, Sweden, Switzerland and the US), is shown in Figure 9.

The results vary hugely by indication, but for eight out of twelve drugs, consumption in the UK is notably below the international average. Needless to say, being 'below average' in any of these categories is not automatically a problem, and being above average is not automatically a good thing. But it illustrates the point that the absence of monetary barriers to access does not mean unimpeded access. The NHS is clearly not an international leader when it comes to providing access to innovative medicines, even if it is ranked as no. 1 in the CF study's 'Cost-Related Access Problems'.

To use an analogy: suppose one pub sells beer at £3.50 a pint, while another pub offers free beer for an evening. In order to limit consumption, the second pub opens later, closes earlier, and understaffs the bar. In order to judge which pub offers better 'access' to beer, we could compare them in terms of per capita beer consumption, perhaps specifically among people on low incomes. The Commonwealth Fund study approach, however, is analogous to asking customers in both pubs whether they had forgone a pint or more on the grounds of cost, and whether they had spent more than £10 on beer. Since nobody in the second pub could answer any of these questions with a 'Yes', the result would be clear right from the start.

Social desirability bias

Some subcategories of the CF study rely on patient surveys, which can be a good thing, because patients' views and experiences are usually underrepresented in outcome-based studies. But some statements to which patients are asked to respond in the CF study leave a lot of room for interpretation, and have no obvious benchmarks, for example (Davis et al. 2014: 19):

- 'Doctor always or often explains things in a way that is easy to understand.'
- 'Specialist always or often involves patient as much as they want in decisions.'
- 'Doctor or health care professional gives clear instructions about symptoms.'

Patients will probably evaluate such statements relative to their expectations, which are inevitably country specific, not relative to some common international standard. This does not mean that they are not relevant, but it limits their suitability for cross-country comparisons.

It is worth noticing that on the questions which leave less room for interpretation, the NHS tends to do less well than the more open-ended questions. This looks suspiciously like an indication of 'social desirability bias'.[9] In the UK, criticism of the NHS is heavily socially discouraged (see, for example, Taylor 2013), so UK responses are probably not easily comparable with those from countries where people feel freer to speak frankly about their health system's shortcomings.

Verdict on the Commonwealth Fund study: useful, but overused

The Commonwealth Fund study is a useful complement to more conventional, outcome-based studies, and shows that there are areas in which the NHS excels. But the trump card status that the study currently enjoys in the UK is unwarranted.

Either way, it only enjoys that status in selected years, namely when it produces the desired result. The Dutch system and the German system, although they have been included less often than the NHS, have both come out on top in previous editions, as Table 5 shows. Yet this was never presented in UK media as 'proof' of the superiority of market-oriented social insurance systems.

The reception of the CF study by NHS supporters is a good illustration of 'motivated reasoning'. As Haidt (2012: 84) explains:

> [W]hen we *want* to believe something, we ask ourselves, '*Can I believe it?*' Then [...] we search for supporting evidence, and if we find even a single piece of pseudo-evidence, we can stop thinking. [...] We have a justification, in case anyone asks.

---

9 'Social desirability bias' is a common problem in opinion surveys about controversial issues, especially when certain views are considered unfashionable or low-status. Broadly speaking, it describes a tendency of respondents to say what they think they are socially expected to say, rather than what they really think. Social desirability bias is probably the main reason why alcohol and tobacco consumption are heavily underreported in consumer expenditure surveys, and why polls failed to predict the UK's 2015 General Election result.

Table 5   The top five in the Commonwealth Fund study, 2004–14

	Year				
Rank	2004	2006	2007	2010	2014
1	New Zealand	Germany*	UK	Netherlands*	UK
2	Australia	New Zealand	Germany	UK	Switzerland*
3	UK	UK	Australia & New Zealand	Australia	Sweden*
4	Canada	Australia	—	Germany	Australia
5	US	Canada	Canada	New Zealand	Germany & Netherlands

*Marks new entries, i.e. countries that have not been included in previous years.
Source: based on Davis et al. (2014).

In contrast, when we *don't* want to believe something, we ask ourselves, '*Must* I believe it?' Then we search for contrary evidence, and if we find a single reason to doubt the claim, we can dismiss it. [...]

Psychologists now have file cabinets full of findings on 'motivated reasoning', showing the many tricks people use to reach the conclusion they want to reach [emphasis in the original].

Spending and efficiency

Efficiency reserves

When defenders of the NHS acknowledge the existence of a gap in health system outcomes between the UK and other countries at all, they tend to blame it on underfunding. This claim has some merit: it is true that by international standards, healthcare spending in the UK is not particularly high. Some of the countries which achieved top results in the comparisons above – France, Sweden, the Netherlands, Germany and Switzerland – spend around 11 per cent of GDP on healthcare, compared with just under 9 per cent in the UK. Two percentage points of GDP is a large difference. The NHS's more acute, recent problems, such as lengthening waiting times for surgery and at A&E departments, can be directly related to financial shortfalls (Appleby et al. 2015). In healthcare as in many other areas, you get what you pay for.

The obvious question then becomes: what would happen to NHS outcomes if UK healthcare spending rose to the levels observed in those countries? Unfortunately, there is no way of knowing. Just as variation in health status is driven by many factors that have nothing to do with the healthcare system as such, so is variation in spending levels. It can be driven by, for instance, differences in demographics, in medical labour market and product market conditions (Feachem et al. 2002), historical legacies, and patient preferences.

The health system efficiency estimates of Joumard et al. (2010) are a comprehensive attempt to disentangle some of the factors at play. The authors model health systems as production functions that turn inputs (healthcare spending, staffing levels) into outcomes (life expectancy, additional life expectancy at age 65, minimised amenable mortality), subject to external constraints (alcohol and tobacco consumption, fruit and vegetable consumption, air pollution, education levels, income levels). Residual cross-country differences in outcomes that the model cannot explain are ascribed to efficiency differences.

The authors express the efficiency reserves of different health systems as potential gains in life expectancy, potential gains in additional life expectancy at age 65, and potential reductions in amenable mortality. These are improvements that could be achieved through a better use of existing resources alone, without improvements in other factors conducive to health. The results are shown in Table 6.

What stands out is that there is no automatic connection between spending levels and efficiency scores. Switzerland and Japan are among the world's biggest healthcare spenders, but they also receive top marks for efficiency. The Irish system, on

Table 6   Efficiency reserves: potential gains in health outcomes
through pure efficiency improvements

Rank	Potential gains in life expectancy		Potential gains in additional life expectancy at age 65		Potential reduction in mortality amenable to healthcare	
1	Australia	≤1 year	Australia	≤1 year	Japan	0–2%
2	Switzerland		Japan		France	
3	South Korea		Switzerland		Italy	
4	Iceland		France		Iceland	
5	Japan		Turkey		South Korea	
6	Mexico	1–2 years	South Korea	1–2 years	Australia	
7	France		Poland		Sweden	2–4%
8	Turkey		Iceland		New Zealand	
9	Portugal		Mexico		Greece	
10	Italy		Canada		Canada	
11	Poland		Spain		Norway	
12	Sweden		Italy		Poland	
13	Spain		Portugal		Mexico	
14	Canada	2–3 years	New Zealand		Spain	
15	Norway		Belgium		Austria	
16	New Zealand		Sweden		Netherlands	
17	Netherlands		Norway		Finland	4–6%
18	Austria		Austria		Luxembourg	
19	Czech Republic		Germany		Portugal	
20	Germany		US	2–3 years	Germany	
21	Belgium		Finland		UK	
22	Ireland	3–4 years	Netherlands		Ireland	
23	Luxembourg		UK		Denmark	6–8%
24	UK		Czech Republic		Czech Republic	
25	Finland		Ireland		US	
26	Greece		Luxembourg		Slovakia	
27	Denmark	4–5 years	Hungary			
28	Slovakia		Greece			
29	Hungary		Denmark			
30	US		Slovakia	3–4 years		

Source: based on Joumard et al. (2010).

the other hand, comes out as one of the least efficient among high-income countries, despite Ireland's comparatively low spending levels. This suggests that, in healthcare, it is possible to spend large sums of money wisely, just as it is possible to spend moderate sums wastefully.

The study also indicates considerable efficiency reserves in the NHS. Life expectancy could be increased by over three years, additional life expectancy at 65 could be increased by over two years, and amenable mortality could be reduced by over 4 per cent through efficiency improvements alone. This does not mean that more money would not help – it almost certainly would. But if the NHS is further away from the 'efficiency frontier' than other Western European systems, then *even if spending levels were identical*, the NHS would still not rise to the standards of its peers.

Voluntary spending

Total healthcare spending in the UK is between one and two percentage points lower than in other northwestern European countries. The gap in *public* healthcare spending, however, is considerably narrower than this (Figure 10). Part of the gap represents voluntary additional spending, which must be related to the fact that most other systems, especially insurance-based systems, make it easier to top up or upgrade statutory healthcare privately. NHS care is more like a take-it-or-leave-it package. Patients cannot easily supplement it privately. For a while, there was even an absolute ban on top-up spending, and while this has since been relaxed, top-ups are still heavily discouraged, and often not possible at all (see Department of Health 2009: 7).

This would not be possible in insurance-based systems. In these systems, the government can, of course, decide that statutory insurance should only cover X and Y but not Z. But it cannot stop or discourage providers from offering Z to willing buyers.

Figure 10 Health expenditure in high-income countries as a % of GDP, 2014 or latest available year

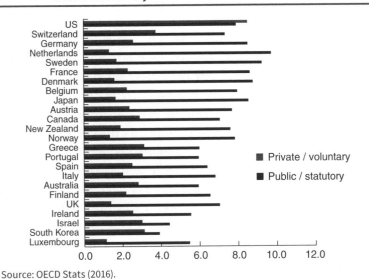

Source: OECD Stats (2016).

In the Swiss and the German system, medical products and services that are not covered by statutory insurance, but which providers routinely offer anyway, are referred to as *Komfortmedizin* ('convenience medicine').[10] For example, statutory insurance covers the cost of hospitalisation in a shared room, but patients can request an upgrade to a double or single bedroom, and pay the extra cost themselves, either out of pocket or through voluntary supplementary insurance (see Stadtspital Triemli (n.d.) for a Swiss example, and Charité Virchow Klinikum (n.d.) for a German example). Other examples would be general anaesthesia for procedures for which local anaesthesia would be sufficient, or,

---

10 Admittedly, *Komfortmedizin* is not a very well-defined term. It can be used in the sense described above, but it is also sometimes used to describe services such as plastic surgery, which are not, strictly speaking 'healthcare' at all. It can refer to services in the border area between healthcare and wellness.

more generally, expensive treatments which are more convenient without being clinically more effective than the standard treatment.

In countries that operate 'reference pricing' systems, top-ups and upgrades are also possible for pharmaceuticals (Drummond et al. 2011). Suppose a drug X costs £1,000. Now a new and enhanced version, X+, is launched for £1,200. In cost-effectiveness appraisals, it turns out that the clinical improvement of X+ relative to X is not large enough to justify the extra £200. This finding will have different implications in different health systems. In the UK, it will normally mean that X+ will not be made available on the NHS. In countries with reference pricing systems, X+ will be available, but it will not be fully reimbursable. The cost of the standard medication X, £1,000, will become the reference price, i.e. the common reimbursement value for both X and X+. But patients can still opt for X+, and pay the extra £200 out of pocket.

Other things equal, a health system which allow top-ups and upgrades will record higher spending levels than a system which does not, without recording commensurately better clinical outcomes. The extras are about comfort, convenience and marginal improvements, not higher survival rates. But it would still be wrong to classify the former system as 'less efficient'. People who pay for those extras do so voluntarily, presumably because they derive some benefit from them. It therefore makes more sense to compare public/statutory spending on healthcare, not total spending. On that count, the UK is still a relatively low spender but it is not exceptional.

In short, the NHS's financial constraints are real, and higher spending would help. But it would not be enough to close the performance gap. The NHS is further away from the efficiency frontier than most other health systems in the developed world, and achieves lower spending in part by making voluntary additional spending difficult.

Robustness to demographic challenges

Healthcare costs rise systematically over people's lifecycle. They are relatively stable during the first five decades or so of life, and begin to rise exponentially afterwards (see Figure 11). On average, per capita healthcare costs for people in the age group between 65 and 74 are almost two and a half times as high as for people aged 16 to 44. For people aged between 75 and 84, that multiple rises to almost four.

Healthcare systems are, in this sense, much like pay-as-you-go financed pension systems, in that most healthcare spending represents a transfer from the working-age generation to the retired generation. In societies where the ratio of the latter to the former (the old-age dependency ratio) is rising, healthcare systems run into the same sustainability problems as PAYGO pension systems. In the UK, there are currently about 28 people aged 65 and over for every 100 people of working age (16–64). That figure is forecast to rise to 47 by 2064 (based on OBR 2015). The share of people aged 85 and over is forecast to rise from today's 4 for every 100 people of working age to 13 (ibid.).

Figure 11 **Healthcare spending per capita by age, as a multiple of those aged 16–44**

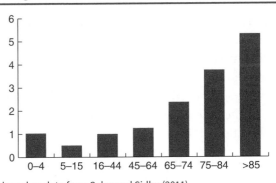

Source: based on data from Caley and Sidhu (2011).

The size of the effect of population ageing on healthcare costs is a matter of dispute. Some studies suggest that ageing in isolation only accounts for around one tenth of the increase in healthcare spending observed in recent decades (OECD 2015: 32–33 and 55–57). Other studies, however, suggest that ageing accounts for a much larger share, possibly around half, of spending increases. According to an estimate specific to the UK, ageing will add about two thirds of a percentage point to the growth rate of healthcare costs in the years until 2031 (Caley and Sidhu 2011). This estimate refers to the *net* effect of ageing; it is already corrected for the fact that the factors which increase longevity also have cost-decreasing effects.[11]

The Office for Budget Responsibility forecasts only moderate increases in NHS spending as a proportion of GDP for the next half century. But this forecast is predicated on the assumption that the NHS will double its long-term productivity growth rate (OBR 2015: 94–97). The OBR does not explain where this sudden productivity upsurge is supposed to come from. They acknowledge, however, that their forecast is highly sensitive to changes in productivity assumptions, and that if NHS productivity growth remained unchanged, NHS spending would rise to over 13 per cent of GDP over the next half century.

We are not in a position to judge which estimate for the effect of ageing, or which productivity scenario, is most plausible. But it is safe to say that ageing is not cost neutral, and that in the future, the healthcare costs of a relatively larger economically inactive population will have to be borne by a relatively smaller economically active population. This will make it necessary to either substantially raise the tax burden on the working-age population, cut back on healthcare entitlements, or hike the retirement age (or some combination of these).

---

11 If average life expectancy in 2031 will be measurably higher than today, then a 75-year-old person in 2031 will typically be in a better state of health than a 75-year-old person today, so their healthcare needs will be lower.

The problem with the latter two options is that, ironically, the same population ageing process which makes these measures economically more pressing also makes them politically less likely to happen. An increase in the old-age dependency ratio also means an increase in the political power of the 'grey vote', and thus in the ability of the retired generation to block fiscal changes unfavourable to them. This effect can be demonstrated in pension policy (Booth 2008), and there is no reason why it should not also apply to healthcare. The first option may be politically more feasible, but it is already hitting economic limits: there is good evidence to suggest that the UK is not too far away from reaching its maximum taxing capacities (Smith 2007, 2011; Minford and Wang 2011). And yet, something will have to give.

The fundamental problem is the absence of old-age reserves in the system. When cost increases are predictable, it makes sense to prepare for them in advance. The fact that healthcare costs are systematically skewed towards the later stages of the life-cycle implies that it would be economically sensible to prefund them: to have a system in which people build up a pot of savings in younger years, and run it down in old age. This could be done individually via medical savings accounts (MSAs), or it could be done by insurers on behalf of their clients, or, in a tax-funded system like the NHS, it could be done by a public agency.

Prefunding expenditure does not just change their timing; moving from a PAYGO system to a prefunded one would mean more than just antedating future expenditure. Firstly, the deadweight loss associated with taxation rises more than linearly with the rate of tax (Feldstein 1995). The deadweight loss of, for example, a 40 per cent tax rate is therefore more than twice as large as the deadweight loss of a 20 per cent tax rate. Prefunding minimises the deadweight loss by smoothing tax levels over time.

Secondly, in a prefunded system, the capital accumulated to meet future healthcare needs would earn a rate of return. PAYGO systems also generate an 'implicit' rate of return, but in developed countries with low birth rates, prefunded systems are almost guaranteed to be more lucrative (Booth and Niemietz 2014: 25–26). Thirdly, other things equal, an economy with a prefunded system will be an economy with a higher rate of savings and investment, leading to a larger capital stock and higher productivity (ibid.: 27–29).

The prefunding issue will be explored in greater detail below. For now, suffice it to say that the NHS has incurred, and continues to incur, huge future liabilities, without setting aside any funds to meet them. Had the NHS been set up on a prefunded basis right from the start, it would now be in command of an old-age reserve fund worth several hundred billion pounds. It would thus be far more resilient to demographic pressures in the coming decades. As things stand, the NHS has no old-age reserves whatsoever.

This is by no means a specifically British problem. The demographic 'time bomb' of increasing longevity and low birth rates is, with differences in degree, common to all developed countries. Healthcare spending is projected to increase in all developed countries for which projections are available (OECD 2015: 29–31). And while the principle of prefunding is well established in theory (see, for example, Feldstein 1999; Stabile and Greenblatt 2010; Robson 2002; Felder 2003), real-world examples of prefunded healthcare are still extremely rare. This means that in this respect, we cannot say that the NHS is doing any worse than other health systems.

Choice and accountability

The OECD tries to quantify the degree of patient choice between providers on a scale from 0 to 6 (Joumard et al. 2010). The notion of 'choice', of course, can be somewhat hollow in a system without a diversified provider sector. It therefore makes sense to also consider the degree of independent sector involvement, as a

Table 7 Degree of patient choice and private sector involvement

	Patient choice	
Private provision	Low (≤4)	High (≥4.5)
Low (≤2)	Finland Spain Portugal New Zealand UK	Iceland Italy Sweden
High (≥3)	Denmark Austria Greece	Switzerland Belgium South Korea Netherlands Australia Germany France Japan Luxembourg Norway

There is no particular reason for the choice of the cut-off values for 'high' and 'low'. They have simply been chosen in such a way that there are enough countries in each category, and that not many countries are too close to the borderline.
Source: based on Joumard et al. (2010).

proxy for pluralism on the provider side. A measure of this, on the same scale, is also available from the OECD. The NHS does not score exceptionally low on either measure, but it remains part of the international 'laggard group' (see Table 7).

We could, of course, argue that it is unfair to judge the NHS, built on a communitarian ethic, by individualistic criteria such as freedom of choice and pluralism. According to Fotaki (2007: 1061):

Choice is central to market liberalism and is firmly rooted in neo-classic economics, given its focus on property rights, individual freedom, competition and user autonomy .... It is a concept [...] traditionally opposed to collectivist values such as equity and the supremacy of community-defined needs where individual choice is not as important.

Critics and supporters of the NHS have always had fundamentally different visions of choice, autonomy and accountability. Its critics see the NHS as a hierarchical, centralised, top-down organisation, which empowers senior healthcare bureaucrats and the medical establishment, but disempowers individual patients. Supporters, however, see it as a grassroots organisation, which is owned and run jointly by 'the people'. Perhaps the best expression of this latter sentiment is the frequent use of the possessive pronoun: *our* NHS, not *the* NHS. From this perspective, the focus on individual choice is missing the point. We do make choices in healthcare – just not in our role as individuals. We make choices in the public sphere – in our role as voters and citizens, as stakeholders in the health service, and as participants in the public debate about healthcare. From this point of view, a greater role for the independent sector, or even an increase in patient choice, actually undermines 'real' choice, by diminishing the public sphere.

This mindset is expressed by, for example, 'Our NHS', one of the many campaign groups fighting against (actual and imaginary) market-oriented health reforms. Among many other things, 'Our NHS' opposes the idea of turning NHS facilities into staff-owned mutuals, cooperatives or social enterprises, on the grounds that 'We all already own the NHS – the latest "mutual" spin is about taking it out of our hands'.[12] The group argues that:

> the government has created new ways to marketise and privatise the health economy – extending personal health budgets, patient choice, piecemeal outsourcing, 'commissioning', and private or 'social' investment. Mutuals and 'social enterprises'

---

12 'We all already own the NHS – the latest "mutual" spin is about taking it out of our hands'. *Our NHS*, 15 July 2014 (https://www.opendemocracy.net/ournhs/caroline -molloy/we-all-already-own-nhs-latest-mutual-spin-is-about-taking-it-out-of-our -hands).

are a key new pathway to market-based services. [...] There is a loss of direct democratic control and accountability.[13]

But the idea that, 'we', 'the people', run things together, as one huge community, is a romantic fantasy. As Seldon (2004 [1990]: 179) explained:

[T]he notion that 'society as a whole' can control 'its productive resources' is common in socialist writing but is patently unrealistic. The machinery of social control has never been devised. There is no conceivable way in which the British citizen can control the controllers of 'his' state railway or NHS, except so indirectly that it is in effect inoperative.

The state-owned industries of the past nominally belonged to 'the people', but apparently, not many people felt that these industries were truly 'theirs'. This is acknowledged even by Owen Jones (2014: 305), who advocates a re-nationalisation of the industries privatised in the 1980s and 1990s:

Thatcher was able to privatize [...] with little popular outcry, because of the lack of a sense of shared ownership among the population. To many, once publicly owned assets [...] seemed remote, run by faceless apparatchiks.

Jones believes that all it would take to turn industries 'run by faceless apparatchiks' into true 'people's industries' is a few organisational tweaks, such as representation of workers and consumers on company boards. But the problems with large-scale collective decision-making are intrinsic. A nationalised industry

---

13 'Should we turn the NHS into co-ops and mutuals?' *Our NHS*, 14 November 2013 (https://www.opendemocracy.net/ournhs/dexter-whitfield/should-we-turn-nhs -into-co-ops-and-mutuals).

is not like the local sports club, where a small number of members, who all have similar interests and who are all passionate about the subject, can meaningfully make decisions together. Quite understandably, most people are not hugely interested in the technical details of the day-to-day running of a steel mill, or, for that matter, a hospital. 'Consumers' and 'workers' are not homogeneous groups with homogeneous interests. It is not an accident that nationalised industries end up being run by 'faceless apparatchiks', and that public participation remains limited to vocal single-issue groups with more concentrated and homogeneous interests. In Seldon's (2004 [1990]: 210) words:

> What belongs nominally to everyone on paper belongs in effect to no-one in practice. Coalfields, railways, schools and hospitals that are owned 'by the people' are in real life owned by phantoms. No nominal owner can sell, hire, lend, bequeath or give them to family, friends or good causes. Public ownership is a myth and a mirage. It is the false promise and the Achilles' heel of socialism. The effort required to 'care' for the 50-millionth individual share of a hospital or school owned by 50 million people, even if identifiable, would far outweigh the benefit; so it is not made, even if it could be. The task is deputed to public servants answerable to politicians who in turn are in socialist mythology answerable to the people. In this long line of communication the citizen is often in effect disenfranchised.

Healthcare is no exception, which is why the rhetoric of 'democratic accountability' always remains at the highest level of theoretical abstraction. Those who make that case never spell out, in more tangible terms, what it actually means in practice. They identify no specific mechanisms, and produce no examples, of 'the people' making decisions. And they could not, because it does not happen. A simple comparison of the healthcare policies that political parties outline in their election manifestos, and the healthcare policies they actually implement once they have won an election, shows that the overlap is virtually zero. Of the major changes in health policy enacted since (at least) 1990, not a single one was announced in the respective governing party's manifesto in the preceding election (Niemietz 2015d: 35–43). The most favourable spin we could put on the idea of 'democratic accountability' is that we could interpret every general election in which a governing party was re-elected as a post-hoc ratification of that party's health policies. Even this interpretation requires courageous assumptions, namely that health policy is decisive among the package of issues that decide election outcomes, and that most voters are aware of the health policies pursued by different parties.

The short summary, then, is that a hypothetical notion of 'collective choice' is *not* a substitute for the very real and concrete choice that a specific patient makes in a specific situation between specific alternatives. The NHS is not a choice-free environment. As we will see in the next chapter, the scope of patient choice has been extended substantially since the early 2000s, and if we could rank health systems by how fast they have travelled in the direction of greater choice, the NHS might well end up in the top group. However, many other health systems remain well ahead of it in this respect.

Conclusion

The NHS remains an international laggard in terms of health outcomes. Survival rates for the most common types of cancer are several percentage points behind those achieved by the best performers. The same is true for strokes, as well as for the more holistic measure of amenable mortality. Waiting times are also longer.

The Commonwealth Fund study is the only one that puts the NHS ahead of other systems overall, but even in this study, the

NHS comes second to last in the category related to health outcomes. The other categories of the study are mainly about inputs and procedures, and some subcategories systematically favour NHS-type systems by design.

NHS spending is lower than healthcare spending in most neighbouring countries, but this does not indicate superior efficiency: in more direct comparisons of efficiency, the NHS comes out in the bottom third of the list. Part of the reason for the relatively low spending figures is simply that the NHS, unlike many other health systems, suppresses voluntary spending. The complete lack of any old-age reserves also means that the NHS is poorly prepared to cope with the demographic pressures that lie ahead, although this is not a specific weakness of the NHS; it is also true of other health systems in the developed world (and, increasingly, in middle-income countries).

And yet, it is not all doom and gloom. In snapshot comparisons, the NHS performance is almost always somewhere between poor and mediocre. But this conceals a time trend of catch-up growth. Figure 12 illustrates this for standardised mortality rates for ischaemic stroke, one of the most important performance measures because it affects so many people: over 120,000 cases are recorded every year in the UK. We have seen above that on this indicator, Sweden, Germany and Switzerland are among the twelve best performers in the world. The time series, however, also shows that these countries already had low stroke mortality rates years ago, and have shown little further improvement over time.[14] The UK, in contrast, has cut its death rate by nearly six percentage points in just a few years. This is not unique – the Netherlands has also shown large recent improvements – and we cannot count on this trend to continue, but it is remarkable nonetheless. A similar pattern can be seen for other indicators.

---

14 This is not because they have reached a natural lower bound. The world's very top performers, Japan, the US and South Korea, show mortality rates below 4 per cent.

Figure 12 Ischaemic stroke 30-day mortality rates (age/sex-standardised), 2000 (or first available year) – 2014 (or latest available year)

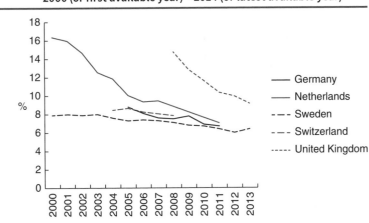

Source: based on OECD Stats (2016).

The next chapter will therefore give an overview of how the NHS has changed in recent years and decades, and what lessons we can learn from previous reforms. This will then directly feed into the reform agenda that will be developed in Chapter 5, an agenda which, for the sake of continuity, will try to build as much as possible on reform processes that have already been started.

3 A QUARTER CENTURY OF NHS REFORMS: WHAT WORKED, WHAT FAILED[1]

It is no exaggeration to say that the Health Service is now under serious threat. [...] The strategy of government ministers has been obvious. Starve the NHS of vital cash and resources then force patients to look to the growing private sector [...] It is clear that had the government carried out a direct onslaught on the NHS the political and public outcry would have been deafening. So their policy has been more subtle, and because of that, more dangerous. There is no doubt in my mind that the NHS is in danger and over the next five years we could find ourselves drifting towards American-type [healthcare].

This quote could easily be from any of today's newspapers. But it is from a 1980 article in *The Times*.[2] Old articles about the imminent demise of the NHS, and about secret plans to privatise it, often have an illusory ring of topicality. The following, from the same newspaper, is another example from 1983:

[The reforms] clear the way for a massive shift of resources from the NHS to private companies. [...] [P]rivate companies (Labour

---

1   This chapter is based on Niemietz (2014, 2015a).

2   The Tory threat to the health service. *The Times*, 1 December 1980.

says) are to be enabled to asset-strip the NHS. [...] [T]he private sector [will] be allowed to pillage NHS resources.[3]

It could easily pass as a current story. Apart from the names, so could this report from the annual conference of the National Association of Health Authorities, published in the same year:

> 'There has been a great deal of talk about hidden manifestoes [sic] and the threat of an attack on the welfare state. That is simply not true', Mr Fowler [the Secretary of State for Social Services] said. [...] His statement did little to convince some of the 500 delegates. [...] Dr Rory O'Moore, chairman of the City and East London Family Practitioner Committee said: 'The health service is up for grabs. [...] [T]he future of the health service [is] open to doubt.'[4]

Or this, from the annual representative meeting of the British Medical Association in 1974: 'Private practice [...] and the possibility of a breakdown of the NHS will dominate discussion'.[5]

Or this one, also from a medical conference, but from as long ago as 1970:

> Dr. Murray [of the Socialist Medical Association] gave a warning that the health service would come under attack from the Tories in government because the service had proved that socialism worked.[6]

Such news stories can be traced back to the NHS's very beginnings.[7] There have always been periodic outbreaks of 'NHS pri-

---

3 Partnership with private sector would help NHS, circular says. *The Times*, 1 June 1983.

4 Renewed pledge on preserving strong NHS. *The Times*, 25 June 1983.

5 Private practice and possibility of NHS breakdown expected to dominate 'doctors' parliament'. *The Times*, 10 July 1974.

6 Private insurance seen as threat to health service. *The Times*, 2 October 1970.

7 Tighter control of health service costs. *The Times* 15 March 1950.

vatisation paranoia', and yet, although the privatisation of the NHS is always 'imminent', it never quite comes about. Spending on healthcare services delivered by non-NHS providers accounts for less than one-tenth of the NHS budget, about £10 billion out of £113 billion (Ham et al. 2015: 17–22). Even then, 'non-NHS' does not automatically mean 'private'. It could refer to services provided by local governments, or organisations that were once part of the NHS and that are now classified as 'independent'.

It would be tempting to jump to the opposite extreme, and conclude that UK healthcare is essentially a reform-free area, in which, although there may be constant reorganisations and re-shufflings within the system, nothing ever changes at the system level. But this would be misleading, too. The past quarter century has seen a number of interesting reform initiatives, and this chapter will evaluate a selection of them.

The purpose of this is not a purely backward-looking one. Before we can outline proposals for future reforms, we first need to establish what has already been tried, and what the results of past reforms have been. It also makes sense for a health reform agenda to build on useful elements of previous reform agendas, both in order to minimise disruption and to avoid unnecessary duplication. We will see that given what has already happened, it is quite unnecessary for health reformers to try to reinvent the wheel. The wheel is already there, but the car needs four of them, and the driver needs to release the handbrake.

The internal market of the 1990s

How it worked

The introduction of market mechanisms into the NHS was first tried in the early 1990s. The idea was to simulate market processes within a state monopoly provider. To this end, the two key functions of the NHS, the allocation of funds and the actual delivery of healthcare services, were separated (the 'purchaser–provider split'). District health authorities (DHAs) became internal commissioners. They were given healthcare budgets from which they were to 'buy' healthcare services from local NHS providers, and they were meant to do so selectively, as a purchaser would do in a real market. Hospitals also became legal entities in their own right ('NHS trusts'), with a degree of autonomy.

DHAs were initially constituted as local monopolies, but a degree of competition was introduced on the purchasing side as well. GPs were given the ability to partly opt out of their DHA's commissioning arrangements, and replace them with their own. These 'general practice fundholders' would be given their own commissioning budgets, with which they would purchase secondary and tertiary healthcare for the patients registered with their practice.

The internal market lacked most of the defining features of an actual market. There was no market-determined entry and exit of providers (Propper et al. 2008: 145). Underperforming hospitals were not allowed to fail, which is why the internal market has been likened to 'the caucus race in Alice in Wonderland, in which "everyone must have prizes"' (Bevan and Hamblin 2009: 162). Well-performing hospitals were constrained in their ability to expand; they were, for example, not allowed to retain budget surpluses. The NHS also remained mostly closed to independent providers (Propper et al. 2004: 1249), and patient choice was not really part of the internal market experiment either. But it was still a break with the cosy competition-free world of the past.

Empirical evidence

Empirical evidence about the impact of the internal market is mixed. GP fundholding was probably the most successful element. Propper et al. (2002) test whether GP fundholders managed to cut hospital waiting times for their patients by optimising referral patterns. They study trends in the waiting times of patients whose GPs became fundholders, relative to the trends in the waiting times of patients whose GPs did not, controlling for patient characteristics. They also study trends in waiting times for treatments commissioned by fundholders, relative to trends in waiting times for treatments over which fundholders had no control.

The authors find that fundholders did achieve shorter waiting times, but the effect was limited to their own patients, and to those treatments over which they had direct control. There is no evidence of positive spillover effects, so fundholding did not speed up hospital access across the board (ibid.: 249):

> Our results indicate that the scheme led to some improvement in the quality of service provided, but only for a limited set of patients and a limited set of treatments. [...] However, because fundholders' patients having non-fundholding procedures did not gain, the overall average waits of fundholders' patients were not significantly less than those of non-fundholders.

The conversion of DHA-managed hospitals into more autonomous NHS trusts was another element of the internal market which seems to have worked well. Söderlund et al. (1997) compare productivity trends between hospitals that were converted into NHS trusts early on, and hospitals that were managed by their DHA for longer, using the latter as a quasi-control group. They find that the conversion was associated with productivity improvements (ibid.: 1127):

> [T]rust status [...] had a significant negative effect on average costs. [...] [O]verall productivity of the hospitals improved over the three years and [...] improvements [...] were significant at the 5% level.

The attempt to create competition between hospitals, on the other hand, backfired. Propper et al. (2004) examine the effect of competition on death rates from acute myocardial infarction, as a proxy for general hospital quality. They split English regions into different bands according to a measure of 'market' concentration, assuming that competition is more intense in regions where concentration is lower, and look at differences in trends for standardised death rates. They find that (ibid.: 1267):

> the impact of competition is to reduce quality. Hospitals located in more competitive areas have higher death rates, controlling for hospital characteristics, actual and potential patient characteristics. [...] [W]hile the estimated impact of competition on quality is small, what it is not is positive.

A similar study by Propper et al. (2008) comes to more nuanced conclusions, showing that competition also has positive effects, namely reductions in waiting times and increased activity levels. But on balance, its impact remains a negative one (ibid.: 165):

> [C]ompetition was associated with significantly lower average waiting times and number of persons on waiting lists. Back-of-the-envelope calculations show that this gain does not, however, offset the fall in quality from higher death rates.

The most likely explanation was the dearth of information on hospital quality that existed at the time. Commissioners could observe waiting lists, prices and a hospital's activity levels, but not quality measures such as standardised mortality rates or infection rates. Hospitals that were faced with competitive pressures shifted their efforts from unobservable to observable outcomes (ibid.: 142):

> [O]utcomes measures such as mortality rates were not publicly available [...] until 1999, two years after the competition

experiment had ended. [...] Thus purchasers had a strong incentive to negotiate lower prices and/or higher volumes but a much weaker incentive to negotiate (and lower ability to observe) quality improvements or even quality maintenance.

At its heart, this 1990s reform disappointed because the preconditions for a functioning market were absent.

The period of 'ultra-managerialism'

How it worked

From 1997 on, the incoming Labour government abandoned most features of the internal market experiment. GP fundholding was abolished, abolishing competition on the commissioner side with it. The mission of commissioning bodies was changed to promoting 'cooperation', not competition, between providers (Mays et al. 2011). Health policy in the first term of the Labour government was marked by a return to the aspiration of providing uniform national standards of care. The 'N' in NHS took centre stage once again.

This period saw the establishment of what is now the National Institute for Health and Care Excellence (NICE), which provides recommendations on whether or not to fund particular treatments on the basis of cost-effectiveness appraisals, of the National Service Frameworks (NSF), which are clinical guidelines aimed at identifying and disseminating medical best practice, and of what is now the Care Quality Commission (CQC), a regulator and inspector of healthcare facilities. All of these organisations have the purpose of reducing regional variation in medical practice and harmonising provision.

From 2000 onwards, in the wake of the publication of the NHS Plan (Department of Health 2000), top-down performance management was intensified. One of the first high-profile measures was the publication of 'star ratings' for NHS trusts. On the one hand, these ratings, based on measures of clinical and financial outcomes, waiting times, patient and staff reviews and so forth, were a reputational device. As Nigel Crisp (2011: 58), the Chief Executive of the NHS at the time, explains:

[W]e gave the service some major top-down shocks to get it moving – primarily through a policy of publicly 'naming and shaming' the worst performers [...] The NHS generally hated it.

But star ratings also had more tangible consequences. Low performers had to put up with inspections and outside interference. Senior management staff could even be sacked on this basis. High performers, meanwhile, were rewarded with greater autonomy and additional investment channelled through a 'performance fund'.

This was taken a step further with the adoption of quantitative performance targets for such outcomes as waiting times and hospital infection rates. Success or failure in meeting these targets was again linked to real consequences in terms of autonomy, investment and so on.

Empirical evidence

The targets/rating system had its shortcomings (Bevan and Hamblin 2009). But it became clear afterwards that the NHS must have had considerable 'fat reserves', which the target system had helped to shed. At the time when the policy was introduced, 80,000 patients had been on a hospital waiting list for more than 15 months, one in five A&E patients waited for more than four hours, and many patients acquired infections in hospitals. The target regime sought to reduce maximum waiting times to 39 weeks in 2005, alongside cutting median waiting times. Ninety-eight per cent of A&E patients were to be treated within four hours, while infection rates were meant to be brought under control at a later stage. All the important targets were met (Crisp 2011: 55–70).

Some of this was the result of Labour's increase in healthcare spending, but the target system also had an independent effect. Hauck and Street (2007) study trends in hospital waiting times in the English–Welsh border region, on the grounds that other factors which might affect outcomes are relatively similar on both sides of the border. The biggest difference between them would be that Wales introduced its target regime later, and applied it less strictly. The authors also take account of the hospitals' overall activity levels and mortality rates, to test whether improvements in waiting lists had simply been achieved by cutting back on the quality and/or quantity of the services provided. They find (ibid.: 288):

> The English hospitals increased levels of activity, reduced length of stay and undertook proportionately more day case activity over the period. Activity levels remained constant at the Welsh hospital, the proportion of day case activity fell, and proportionately more non-elective patients were admitted. There is no evidence that the English hospitals achieved activity increases by compromising on quality. Mortality rates at the English hospitals remained low or declined further over the period, but the high and rising hospital mortality rates at the North East Wales Trust are cause for concern.

The general criticism of centralised control is that the 'central planners' will lack knowledge of local conditions, especially the type of knowledge that cannot easily be expressed in numbers or even words ('tacit knowledge'). The British experience with centralised performance management of the health service amply illustrates the validity of this criticism. But the rapid improvement in measures such as waiting times and infection rates shows that there must have been a fair amount of low-hanging fruit at the time. Plucking this fruit did not even require a lot of local knowledge, just greater pressure to go ahead and pluck it.

The quasi-market reforms of the 2000s

How it worked: patient choice

From 2002 on, market mechanisms slowly began to creep back in again. An important step was the introduction of patient choice. This started with small local pilot projects in 2002. Patients who could not be treated at the hospital they had been referred to within six months were given the option to switch to a hospital with shorter waiting times. At the time, the government still shied away from using the 'neoliberal' language of choice and competition. The pilots were presented as purely a means to reduce waiting times by allocating patients more efficiently.

Early experience with patient choice was positive. Dawson et al. (2007) estimate the effect of the London Patient Choice Project (LPCP) on waiting times. They look at the time trend in waiting times at London hospitals, relative to the national average, to the average for metropolitan areas, and to the average for a more tailor-made control group. The authors find that (ibid.: 119):

> the overall difference in waiting times between LPCP hospitals and the control groups [...] is significant and negative [...] LPCP waiting times were between 3 and 4 weeks shorter.

Choice of an alternative provider after six months was subsequently rolled out nationwide. From 2006 on, it was taken a step further: GPs now had to offer all patients a choice between four or five different providers at the point of referral, and one of these options had to be from the independent sector. In 2008, patient choice at the point of referral was extended to any eligible provider. Choose and Book, an online booking system, and NHS Choices, a website with information on provider performance, were launched simultaneously.

That, at least, was the situation in theory. Implementation on the ground lagged behind, probably because GPs – a majority of which expressed negative views of the reform in surveys (Dixon and Robertson 2011: 54–55) – were slow to adapt. In the first year, only about a third of patients were actually offered a choice by their GP upon referral, a share which rose to about half over the next few years, but later fell back to one third (Ham et al. 2015: 51). Those who were given a choice were usually not given the full range, and private providers in particular were almost never included among those options. So the choices that existed on paper did not fully translate into choices actually experienced by patients. Still, given that the NHS had been a virtually choice-free environment for most of its history, it was a major attempt to shift power from providers to patients.

How it worked: the money follows the patient

Patient choice became meaningful only because it was coupled with a reform of the payment system. Until 2003, NHS hospitals had been paid through annual block contracts, with payments that were only loosely linked to activity levels. Hospitals therefore had no incentive to attract patients and increase activity levels. From then on, the gradual rolling out of an alternative payment system, termed Payment by Results (PbR), began. Payment by Results is a misnomer for a system that should really be called 'Payment by Activity'. The PbR system splits patients into groups on the basis of their diagnosis and assigns a reimbursement level to each group. This level is based on the average cost of the treatment required by patients in the respective diagnosis group, with some adjustment for severity and local variation in wages and prices. In this, the UK followed a broader international trend towards so-called 'diagnosis-related group' (DRG) payment systems of standardised tariffs. The purpose of DRG systems is to incentivise providers to attract more patients, but without incentivising overtreatment or unnecessarily costly treatment for a given patient. Attracting an additional patient would lead to additional revenue, but a longer hospital stay and/or extravagant additional treatments would not.

PbR initially covered only selected treatments in selected hospitals, with the remainder of hospital revenue still coming through the old block contract system. But it was subsequently expanded to more providers and more procedures. By 2006 about 60 per cent of hospital revenue came from PbR payments (Gaynor et al. 2011: 11). Since then, however, implementation has stalled. The original intention was that, at some point, almost all healthcare spending would be allocated through activity-based payment formulas. This has not materialised (Farrar et al. 2011: 68).

How it worked: Foundation Trusts

The third major ingredient in this reform package was the creation of largely self-governing Foundation Trust (FT) hospitals. Hospitals could apply for FT status when they met specified standards of clinical and financial performance ('earned autonomy'). The first conversions to FT status occurred in 2004, and by 2010, 131 NHS hospitals had become FTs (Allen and Jones 2011: 25). But, again, the process stalled. The original intention was that all hospitals would eventually acquire FT status, which has not been achieved.

Even though Labour's health policy developed in a very haphazard way, this package of market-oriented reforms was internally consistent. It created a system in which patients could not just choose providers, but in which the choices patients made had a real impact on providers because the money followed them.

This gave providers a good reason to be responsive to patients' needs. In this context, the introduction of FT status also became sensible: now that providers were more directly accountable to their patients, government interference with their day-to-day operations became less necessary.

Primary Care Trusts

Even though the internal market officially came to an end in 1997, the purchaser–provider split remained. In a sense, it was even strengthened with the creation of independent local commissioning bodies, the Primary Care Trusts (PCTs). PCTs took over the functions from local and district health authorities. They were supposed to actively shape the delivery of healthcare, even if this meant challenging providers and established practices. One of the main motivations was to achieve more integrated, coordinated care, and to deliver healthcare in a more decentralised manner. PCTs were meant to convert a provider-led into a commissioner-led system, and to decrease what was seen as an overreliance on the hospital sector.

The Private Finance Initiative

The Private Finance Initiative (PFI) is a form of public–private partnership under which private companies build and maintain new healthcare facilities (for example, a new hospital ward) for an NHS trust, and then lease them to that trust for an annual fee. The first PFI facility was opened in 2000, and thirteen years later, there were 118 PFI projects at various stages of completion, managing a combined capital value of £11.6 billion (European Commission 2013). PFI contracts usually run for 25 years, and sometimes longer.

Of all of the reforms of the 2000s, PFI was probably the most controversial one, and certainly the most emblematic. The press coverage has been almost unanimously negative:[8] PFI is commonly presented as a fraudulent scheme by which private corporations drain the NHS of valuable resources. For the purposes of this monograph, however, PFI is the least interesting reform of the 2000s. While often presented as an excess of 'free market ideology', PFI was nothing of the sort.

Firstly, under PFI, private companies are not allowed anywhere near the provision of healthcare. They manage only the premises within which healthcare is provided. But more importantly, support for, or opposition to, PFI is not a state-versus-market matter. It is a matter of outsourcing versus in-house provision. Sometimes it makes sense for an NHS trust (or any other organisation) to purchase a service from an external provider (examples include cleaning, IT, catering, accountancy and recruitment), sometimes it makes more sense to employ staff in-house for those jobs. This will depend on local factors specific to the organisation and the environment in which it operates. The construction and management of a healthcare facility falls into the same category; it only differs from the other examples in scale and time horizon. How one judges the relative merits of market provision and state provision is completely irrelevant in this context.

PFI is only included here because it is a high-profile subject. Conceptually, it should not be considered part of the quasi-market reforms. A market reform would have devolved such questions to individual hospital trusts. But a system of state hospital planning, in which the central government decides which hospital facilities should expand, and in what way, is not a market system, even if

---

8   The PFI hospitals costing NHS £2bn every year. *The Telegraph*, 18 July 2015. Crippling PFI deals leave Britain £222bn in debt. *The Independent*, 11 April 2015. Corbyn's right. PFI is an unaffordable mistake for the NHS. *The Guardian*, 28 August 2015. To save the NHS, Labour must face the ugly truth of PFI debts. *New Statesman*, 10 July 2014. How PFI is crippling the NHS. *The Guardian*, 29 June 2012. Counting the cost of PFI in the national health service. *Channel Four News*, 26 June 2012.

it involves some private companies. To put it bluntly: if the government of North Korea decided to outsource the construction and maintenance of a military facility to a private company from South Korea, then this would not make North Korea 'neoliberal'.

Empirical evidence

A number of studies have investigated the impact of choice-driven competition on the quality and efficiency of hospital care (see, for example, Bevan and Skellern 2011). These studies map the degree of potential competition between hospitals in different parts of England, applying standard measures of industry concentration to the hospital sector. The least competitive areas are then treated as a quasi-control group. The time trend in outcomes in these areas is interpreted as the closest thing to what the time trend in England as a whole would have been if the reforms had never happened. Studies also attempt to control for factors that are thought to be associated with competition without being causally related to it, alongside differences in case mix and case severity.

In this way, Bloom et al. (2010) study the relationship between the intensity of competition and the quality of hospital care, approximated by mortality rates from acute myocardial infarction (AMI) and emergency surgery. They find that (ibid.: 14):

> hospitals facing more competition have significantly fewer deaths following emergency AMI admissions. [...] [T]here appears to be a causal effect whereby adding one extra hospital reduces death rates by 1.83 percentage points.

They also find that competition lowers the death rate from emergency surgery.

Gaynor et al. (2011) estimate differences in time trends for AMI, as well as all-causes mortality rates, again comparing hospitals facing varying degrees of competition. Their results show that (ibid.: 20–21):

> higher market concentration (a larger HHI[9]) leads to lower quality. A 10 per cent increase in the HHI leads to an increase of 2.91 per cent in the AMI death rate. [...] The estimate [for the all-cause mortality rate] again shows a significant relationship between quality and market concentration. [...] This amounts to [...] a little over 8 fewer AMI deaths annually per hospital, or approximately 1,000 fewer total deaths per year over all 135 hospitals in our sample.

The authors show that the better performance of hospitals exposed to competition is not a continuation of a previously existing trend, but a new trend that started when competition became effective.

In a similar model, which also uses the difference-in-differences in AMI death rates as a proxy for hospital quality, Cooper et al. (2011: 244) find:

> 30-day AMI mortality fell 0.31 percentage points faster per year after the reforms for patients treated in more competitive markets [...] Framed differently, the shift from a market with two equally sized providers to one with four equally sized providers after the reforms would have resulted in a 0.39 percentage point faster reduction in AMI mortality per year from 2006 onwards.

These researchers, too, rule out the possibility that this was merely a continuation of a pre-existing trend, or an artefact of how 'competitiveness' was measured (ibid.: 244–45):

---

9 Herfindahl–Hirschman Index, a measure of market concentration which is widely used in industrial economics.

> An essential observation [...] is that the pre-policy trend in AMI mortality in areas with uncompetitive market structures is not statistically different from the trend in markets with competitive structures once we control for patient characteristics [...] Our findings remain consistent and significant across the seven different measures of market structure.

Models of this type have also been used to study the relationship between competition and hospital efficiency. The paper by Gaynor et al. (2011) uses average length of stay (ALOS) as a proxy for efficiency, alongside information on hospital expenditure per activity. The authors find that hospitals in more competitive markets have recorded greater productivity improvements (ibid.: 22):

> The estimated coefficient implies that a 10 per cent fall in a hospital's HHI on average results in a 2.3 per cent fall in length-of-stay. [...] Taken together, the findings for quality [...] and resource utilization [...] suggest that hospitals facing more competitive pressure were able to find ways to marshal resources more efficiently to produce better patient outcomes.

Cooper et al. (2012) use a similar model. They test whether ALOS reductions represent genuine efficiency improvements or whether they have been achieved by discharging patients sooner than is clinically appropriate. They split ALOS into a pre-surgery component and a post-surgery component, arguing that the former (the time from a patient's arrival at the hospital to the commencement of the procedure) can only be shortened by genuine improvements in the hospital's internal workflow. Their findings (ibid.: 18):

> [A] one standard deviation decrease in market concentration pre-reform was associated with a reduction in overall LOS [length of stay] of between 2 per cent and 6 per cent relative to

the mean LOS over that period. [...] Framed differently, the addition of one hospital to a hospital market lowered the LOS for patients treated in that area by approximately 0.4 days.

However, the authors also found that the inclusion of private hospitals has a negative effect on the productivity of nearby public hospitals. Their explanation is that the latter probably attract patients who are generally healthier, but in ways which the control variables fail to register (and the PbR severity adjustments fail fully to compensate for).

Some studies have also taken a closer look at the transmission mechanisms behind these results, exploring not just *whether* but also *how* competition has driven up standards.

One part of the answer is that once they were able to exercise choice in a meaningful way, patients became more discriminating and quality conscious. Gaynor et al. (2011: 19) argue that:

> If patients became more responsive to quality post-policy we should see better hospitals (those in the bottom quartile of the mortality distribution) attracting more patients relative to worse hospitals (those in the top quartile). That is exactly what the data show ... [T]he share of patients bypassing their nearest hospital increased for better hospitals while it clearly decreased for worse hospitals. This provides reassurance that there is a patient response to quality and that it increased during the reform.

A study by Gaynor et al. (2012) examines patient behaviour in greater detail. For patients undergoing coronary artery bypass graft surgery, they estimate whether hospitals that record low (high) standardised mortality rates experience an increase (decrease) in demand in subsequent years (the elasticity of demand with respect to quality). They find that before the introduction of choice, when patient demand was mediated through GPs' decisions, the elasticity of demand was indistinguishable from zero. After the introduction of choice, it fell to −0.12: patients did discriminate against underperforming hospitals.

The authors also estimate how a hospital's mortality rate affects its market share in subsequent years. In the pre-reform period, an increase in the mortality rate by one standard deviation would only reduce a hospital's market share by 0.36 per cent. After the reform, though, the same increase in mortality would be punished with a 4.9 per cent loss in market share (ibid.: 24). Sicker patients were more responsive to quality differences than healthier ones, as we would expect given that more is at stake for them. Income, on the other hand, was a poor predictor of responsiveness.

Also looking at transmission channels through which competition affects quality, Bloom et al. (2010) study the relationship between competition and an index of management quality. This index measures the extent to which formalised procedures of quality control, monitoring, reporting, accountability, and so on, are in place. The authors show that hospitals that are 'better managed' according to their indicator also record lower mortality rates, shorter waiting lists, lower MRSA infection rates, higher operating margins, and higher levels of job satisfaction among employees (ibid.: 11–12, 23). They also find that management quality is, among other factors, driven by competition.

The quasi-market reforms can also go some way towards explaining the performance gap between the English NHS and its counterparts in Wales and Scotland, which have been much more hesitant to introduce market mechanisms. Despite higher levels of per capita spending and higher staffing levels, the Welsh and the Scottish NHS trail behind the English NHS on most outcome measures, while also showing lower activity levels (Bevan et al. 2014). Perhaps the most important difference is the gap in amenable mortality between Wales and Scotland on the one hand, and the North of England, a region which is similar to Scotland and Wales in socio-economic terms, on the other.

Unsurprisingly, NHS 'purists' who were opposed to the quasi-market reforms right from the start have not changed their minds in the light of the evidence. Pollock et al. (2012) have dismissed what they call the 'drip feed of pro-competition studies' as ideologically motivated 'bad science'. Their objections, however, mostly reiterate minor methodological points that the authors of these 'pro-competition studies' have already dealt with at length.

For example, Pollock et al. argue that AMI survival rates cannot serve as a proxy for the effect of competition and choice, because people who have suffered a heart attack obviously do not 'choose' a hospital, and hospitals do not 'compete' for these patients. This is, of course, correct, but it is not a weakness of the studies. It is a strength. Suppose the positive effect of competition could only be shown for treatments that are particularly amenable to choice, i.e. non-urgent elective surgery in areas where outcomes are comparatively easy to judge. We would then have to suspect that providers had merely shifted their efforts from areas which are not subject to competition to areas which are. Yet the fact that we observe clinical improvements even in an unlikely area such as AMI care suggests that the reforms have led to genuine, across-the-board improvements, which have spilled over into areas not directly affected by them.

Coulter (2010) is less dismissive of the evidence, but still maintains that:

> recent studies of the effect of the NHS reforms [...] suggested that certain hospitals in areas where competition is more intense may have succeeded in attracting more patients, reducing preoperative lengths of stay, and reducing mortality, although the mechanisms by which the changes were achieved, and indeed whether there is any causative link between these indicators, remains unclear.

This is true, but it demands impossible standards of the literature.

Pollock et al. (2012) also argue that choice and competition cannot have been the decisive factors driving improvements, because most patients did not even know that they had a choice of provider. But again, this is a strength, not a weakness, of the pro-competition studies. It suggests that even a relatively small dose of choice-based reforms can lead to measurable improvements. The implication would be that extending the reach of the reforms could lead to even larger benefits.

On a related note, Pollock et al. argue that even among patients who did make an active choice, only a small minority based their decision on the information provided by the NHS Choices website. Again, they see this as evidence that choice and competition cannot have been causal factors. Similarly, Coulter (2010) argues that:

> fewer than 1 in 10 [patients were] looking at officially published data on quality and performance. [...] Even in the United States [...] there is little evidence that patients' choices are influenced by published performance data. Nor is it evident that patient choice itself drives up quality standards.

More to the point, Ellis (2013) argues that informed provider choice is

> a difficult matter of data analysis that most people (myself included) would not be qualified to undertake. Have you ever read the reviews on the NHS Choices website? It's largely complaints about rude receptionists and lack of online booking [...] Most patients will end up rolling the dice and hoping they've chosen well. [...] But these things are too important to be left to the free market; for the clever to win on and the stupid to lose.

This is a variation of a line of argument which is common among critics of market mechanisms in healthcare. These critics (e.g.

Godlee 2007, 2012) often start from the 'Econ 101' textbook model of perfectly informed, perfectly rational utility-maximisers, and then go on to highlight the many ways in which real-world behaviour of patients deviates from this model. The mere fact that such discrepancies exist is then presented as evidence that markets could not possibly work in healthcare.

But it is, of course, a common approach in economics to deliberately start from simplistic, unrealistic assumptions, and then relax those assumptions step by step, and test whether the conclusions still hold. An economic model is, in this sense, like a house of cards: some cards cannot be pulled out without the whole house collapsing, but some can quite easily. Critics of markets in healthcare simply *assert* that the pulling of *any* card would lead to the collapse of the house. They see no need to test whether it actually does.

But if we applied their logic to other sectors, we would have to conclude that choice and competition can almost never work in any area. It is tantamount to arguing that computers or washing machines could not possibly be provided by the market, because only a small fraction of the people who buy these products base their decision on hard technical evidence, such as ratings in consumer magazines.

But this is not how competition works. It is not necessary for consumers to behave anything like utility-maximising 'cyborgs'. All it takes is a minority of active consumers, and some moderate correlation between hard evidence and 'softer' indicators of quality, especially a provider's reputation.

In short, the evidence on the quasi-market reforms is overwhelmingly positive, even if it could never be strong enough to convince the die-hard critics. The 2000s were not, however, a 'golden age' of health reform. There is good evidence that Private Finance Initiative (PFI) schemes often represent poor value for money (European Commission 2013: 32; Hurst and Williams 2012: 57). As explained above, though, PFI should not be seen as part of the quasi-market reform programme. PFI meant outsourcing, not marketisation. Those who see it as such seem to define 'marketisation' as 'anything which leads to greater private sector involvement', but this is not a workable definition. Suppose, hypothetically, that NHS trusts were banned from employing their own cleaners and/or IT personnel. They would then be forced to buy those services from private companies, so technically, this would lead to greater private sector involvement. But it would be the very opposite of marketisation, because it would increase the degree of state control over NHS trusts.

Further, the aim of turning a provider-led into a commissioner-led system has not been achieved. The commissioning side has been characterised as relatively weak in the face of strong providers. Studies find that while there are some local examples of commissioners changing healthcare delivery patterns and pathways in their areas, effective commissioning has not become the national norm (Smith and Curry 2011; Ham et al. 2011).

Most of the reform elements, even if successful as far as they went, have stalled, or not been pursued with much vigour. The conversion of hospitals into Foundation Trusts, the shift towards activity-based payments, the rolling out of patient choice and the involvement of independent sector organisations have been beneficial, but not taken as far as originally envisaged.

Perhaps the biggest mistake, though, was the policy zigzag of the period from, roughly, 1997 to 2003. Broadly speaking, during that period, the government first abolished the internal market created by its predecessor, and then started to build its own version of it half a decade later. This meant that several years of reform effort were wasted, and that health reform became unnecessarily disruptive. It would have been far more sensible to build on what was already there. The internal market of the 1990s had major flaws, but these could have been addressed within the inherited setup.

Disruption is probably inevitable when there are genuine ideological differences between governments, leading to genuinely different objectives for health policy. But this was manifestly not the case here. The internal market of the 1990s and the quasi-market of the 2000s were cut from the same theoretical cloth, namely the theories of 'managed competition', as developed by economists Alain Enthoven (Timmins and Davies 2015: 68) and Julian Le Grand (Le Grand 2003: 95–106). It would therefore clearly have been possible to secure policy continuity.

Recent reforms

The more recent health policy changes, enacted under the Liberal-Conservative coalition, and later, the Conservative majority government, have been highly controversial, but from the perspective of this monograph, they have not been particularly interesting. The 2012 Health and Social Care Act (HSCA) and related changes neither extended the Labour government's quasi-market reforms in a substantive way, nor did they roll them back.

The biggest change was the slowdown in spending increases. The 2000 NHS Plan had contained a pledge to increase UK healthcare spending to the Western European average, and by 2010, that promise had been largely fulfilled. From then on, fiscal consolidation became a policy priority, and the real-terms increase in NHS spending slowed down from an average of more than 5 per cent per annum to less than 1 per cent (Appleby et al. 2015: 5–8).

On an organisational level, the biggest change brought about by the HSCA was the abolition of Primary Care Trusts (PCTs). Responsibilities for commissioning healthcare were split between newly formed local Clinical Commissioning Groups (CCGs), a national commissioning board (NHS England), and local authorities (Ham et al. 2015). CCGs were meant to be led by GPs (although their governance structure became more complicated), echoing the earlier model of GP fundholding, which had been part of the 1990s internal market. As always, critics interpreted this reorganisation of the commissioning side as an attempt to 'privatise the NHS'. But even the King's Fund, which was among the HSCA's most outspoken critics, described these claims as a red herring (ibid.: 22):

> Arguments about privatisation distract from the much more important and damaging impacts of the reforms on [...] the ability [...] to deal with rapidly growing financial and service pressures. By taking three years to dismantle the old structures and reassemble them into new ones, the government took scarce time and expertise away from efforts to address these pressures. [...] it seems likely that the massive organisational changes that resulted from the reforms contributed to widespread financial distress and failure to hit key targets for patient care.

The most high-profile events in recent years must have been the junior doctors' strikes and the conflicts leading up to them. This was again widely interpreted to be, somehow, about 'privatisation' of the NHS. As Owen Jones described it:

> [A]sk a striking junior doctor why they're taking this action, and you won't simply hear an eloquent spiel about their contracts. It's the very future of the NHS – which they have committed their lives to – which they fear is at stake. There are the government's policies of marketisation [...] stripping the 'national' from NHS.[10]

But for all the motives that may have been projected onto it, the junior doctors' strikes were essentially just glorified industrial disputes. They had nothing to do with 'marketisation'. A system in which a government department is directly involved in

---

10 Junior doctors are striking for us all – to save the NHS and to make a stand. *The Guardian*, 12 January 2016.

negotiating salaries, working hours and other work conditions is self-evidently not a market system. A market-oriented reform in this area would have ended the Department of Health's involvement in negotiating employment contracts altogether, and devolved such matters to individual hospitals, surgeries and CCGs.

Conclusion

The creation of the internal market in the 1990s was the first attempt to introduce market mechanisms into the NHS. It had some successful elements. The model of 'GP fundholding', under which GPs could became healthcare commissioners, led to shorter hospital waiting times for patients registered with fundholding GPs, at least in the areas to which the model was applied. It also seems to have led to a more efficient use of resources. The greater independence that came with the conversion of NHS hospitals, which used to be part of the wider health bureaucracy, into standalone trusts, also led to small improvements in efficiency. But its main component, competition between hospitals, failed during this period. A higher degree of competition was associated with worse clinical outcomes.

The subsequent period of centralised performance management, while not a permanent solution, did succeed in tackling some of the more obvious 'fat reserves' in the system, by putting some much-needed pressure on providers. The target system encouraged gaming the system, and it distracted from local priorities, but it also brought some real improvement in waiting times and patient safety. A positive legacy of the era was that reliable information on provider performance was now widely available.

From 2002 on, market mechanisms slowly began to creep back in. A new payment system in which money follows patients was gradually introduced, patients were given choice of provider at the point of referral, and providers were given greater autonomy. There were also efforts to strengthen the role of commissioners, and to make greater use of private capital in the building and maintenance of new healthcare facilities.

The empirical evidence of this 'quasi-market' reform period is overwhelmingly positive. Hospitals that were exposed to a greater degree of competition recorded greater improvements in clinical outcomes, financial outcomes and efficiency measures. Some patients bypassed underperforming hospitals nearby in favour of better-performing ones further away, so the latter gained market shares at the expense of the former.

But plans to shift power from providers to commissioners, and in this way, to develop more integrated patterns of healthcare delivery, as well as greater subsidiarity, have so far been unsuccessful. Most reform efforts have stalled at some point: not all hospitals have been converted into Foundation Trusts, not all of their revenue is channelled through the Payment by Results system, and not all GPs inform their patients about their right to choose providers.

A persistent problem has been the lack of policy continuity. In 1997, the New Labour government began to dismantle the internal market they inherited, only to start building its own version of it half a decade later. Similarly, in 2012, the Liberal–Conservative coalition government began to dismantle the established commissioning structure, and build a new one from scratch, with no obvious benefits. The quasi-market reforms which the coalition inherited were very much unfinished business. But rather than just finishing the job, and working within the existing structures, the coalition embarked on yet another huge reorganisation exercise.

Chapter 5 will draw on these lessons, and develop an agenda for building on the quasi-market reforms. First, however, the next chapter will broaden the perspective. While this chapter has had a very domestic focus, the next one will complement this by taking a look abroad. Compared to its own past, today's NHS looks like a relatively patient-centric, pluralistic and competitive system. Compared to other modern health systems, however, it looks much less so. There are plenty of countries where patients enjoy a much greater degree of freedom, and where the provider side is a lot more diversified and competitive than in the UK. The quasi-market reforms made a difference, but they started from a low base.

4 OTHER GAMES IN TOWN[1]

The NHS debate: insular and inward-looking

The last general election campaigns were characterised by an appetite for learning from international best practice. All major political parties showed a curiosity for reform ideas which had worked, or were perceived to be working, elsewhere. The UK's 'free schools', for example, were directly inspired by the Swedish *friskolor*.

Healthcare, however, has remained completely untouched by this trend. The only foreign healthcare system that is occasionally mentioned in the British debate is the American one, and then only in a self-congratulatory way, because that system's well-known flaws make it an easy target. The healthcare debate remains insular and inward-looking, seemingly oblivious to any developments elsewhere.

The result is that the British healthcare debate is, in some ways, completely 'out of sync' with debates in otherwise similar countries, even if these countries' health systems are built on similar values and face similar challenges. Several policy ideas, which are solidly part of the mainstream debate in most neighbouring countries, are considered beyond the pale in the UK.

---

1   This chapter is based on Niemietz (2015b). Unless otherwise indicated, information on the Dutch system is taken from Schäfer et al. (2010), and information on the Swiss system is taken from European Observatory on Health Care Systems (2000) and Daley and Gubb (2013).

Figure 13 Public and private shares of hospital provision (% of hospital beds)

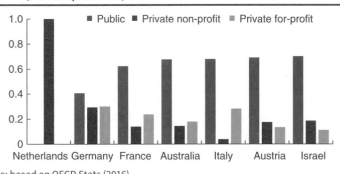

Source: based on OECD Stats (2016).

The most obvious one is private sector involvement in the delivery of healthcare. In Continental Europe, including in countries with strong social democratic traditions, this has long been a reality. In France, Italy and Austria, countries which one could hardly accuse of an exaggerated faith in free markets and private initiative, the private sector accounts for about one third of the hospital sector (Figure 13). Among comparable non-European countries, this is also the case in Australia and Israel. In Germany, private hospital care is the norm, with the private sector supplying three out of every five hospital beds. In the Netherlands, there is no such thing as a 'public hospital' anymore: all hospitals have been converted into (or have always been) private non-profit organisations.

In the UK, by contrast, there has only been one single, short-lived attempt to have an NHS-funded hospital managed (not even owned) by a private company, and even that was enough to cause an outcry.[2] When this company pulled out – the contract

---

2   *The Guardian*, for example: First privately run NHS hospital 'is accident waiting to happen', 10 November 2011; Andrew Lansley's NHS is all about private sector hype, 11 November 2011; Care may suffer, admits private company taking over NHS hospital, 12 November 2011.

had not specified any long-term obligations – BBC Business News presented it as the definitive proof that the private sector cannot run hospitals.[3]

Another example would be co-payments. The majority of developed countries demand some form of cost-sharing either for primary care, or hospital care, or both (Cawston and Corrie 2013: 18). This includes countries such as Sweden, Finland and (for primary care) Norway, which are usually held up as role models to be emulated in British social policy debates. Cost-sharing schemes can conflict with the policy goal of equitable healthcare, but they can also be perfectly compatible with it – it simply depends on how they are designed, and there are huge cross-country differences in design (ibid.: 23). In Sweden, out-of-pocket expenditure accounts for 16 per cent of total health expenditure, compared to 9 per cent in the UK. In Switzerland, it accounts for as much as 26 per cent (based on WHO 2015: 132–33). And yet even in the Commonwealth Fund study, the preferred study of NHS supporters (see Chapter 2), the Swedish system is rated as better than the NHS in the Equity category, and the Swiss system draws level with the NHS (Davis 2014: 23–25). The US system, meanwhile, is rated as the least equitable one, although the share of out-of-pocket payments is no more than 12 per cent. And yet, in the UK, the idea of charging patients for primary or hospital care is outside the 'Overton Window'.[4]

The healthcare debate in the UK would probably be very different if it drew to a greater extent on international experience. This chapter will give a cursory overview of how alternative systems work. For the sake of brevity, it will start by describing a *family*

---

3 Can a private business run a hospital? *BBC Business News*, 9 January 2015.

4 The Overton Window is, roughly, the range of political ideas that can at least be publicly debated, even if they are not necessarily popular. Ideas are outside the Overton Window when most people would immediately dismiss them as extreme, or treat them as self-evidently absurd.

Table 8   The number of UK lives that could be saved if patients were
           treated in other countries' healthcare systems

	Belgium	Germany	Israel	Netherlands	Switzerland
Breast cancer	2,631	2,524	3,598	2,255	n/a
Prostate cancer	4,446	3,784	5,108	1,230	2,270
Lung cancer	3,187	3,005	6,465	2,367	3,141
Bowel cancer	4,440	3,289	5,838	3,207	n/a
Skin melanoma	–279	585	n/a	443	730
Ischaemic stroke	–128	3,570	4,080	2,678	2,933
Haemorrhagic stroke	–135	2,205	1,013	–1,035	1,463
Amenable mortality	10,705	2,692	n/a	13,333	24,038

Source: based on OECD Stats (2016); Allemani et al. (2015); Cancer Research UK (2015); Eurocare (2014); Stroke Association (2016); Eurostat (2015).

of systems rather than an individual system: social health insurance (SHI) systems. The systems of Switzerland, the Netherlands, Germany, Belgium and Israel (which can be considered 'pure' SHI systems) have enough in common to fit into a summary description, and, taken together, they cover over 120 million people. In the rankings presented in Chapter 2, these countries have quite consistently outperformed the NHS.

This is summarised again in Table 8, which shows the number of lives that could be saved if UK patients suffering from various afflictions were treated in SHI countries rather than by the NHS. It also shows the same for amenable mortality, as a summary measure. Negative figures arise when the UK records higher survival rates than the comparator country.

These are, of course, back-of-the-cigarette-packet figures based on survival rates and prevalence numbers that change from year to year, and we should not read too much into small differences. But four-digit figures cannot be dismissed as aberrations.

How social health insurance systems work

Social insurance works, in principle, like conventional private insurance: individuals pay regular contributions to a health insurer of their choice, seek treatment from a medical provider of their choice when they fall ill, and their insurer then reimburses the provider for the expenses incurred. The following features distinguish SHI systems from conventional insurance:

Community rating: in SHI systems, insurers cannot vary premiums in accordance with individual health risks.

Obligation to accept/contract: in SHI systems, insurers cannot reject applicants on the basis of their medical history, family history or other predictors of risk.

No exclusion clauses: in SHI systems, insurers cannot rule out coverage for pre-existing conditions. They must offer the full package to every applicant.

Individual mandate: in SHI systems, everybody is obliged to purchase a basic insurance package, specified by the government, for themselves and their dependants. People who do not do so are signed up automatically, even against their will.[5]

Premium subsidies: as a logical correlate of the former point, in SHI systems the government subsidises the health insurance premiums of people on low incomes. This can be done through a means-tested subsidy, as in Switzerland, or by making all premiums income-dependent, as in Germany.

---

5   The Netherlands offers exemptions for people who oppose insurance for religious reasons.

Table 9   Risk structure compensation: a stylised example

	Insurer X		Insurer Y			
	Person A		Person B		Person C	
Baseline healthcare costs (= insurance premium under community rating)	€500		€500		€500	
Individual risk factors:						
Age	20 years	–€50	20 years	–€50	70 years	+€150
Chronic conditions	none	–€100	none	–€100	Thyroid disorder	+€200
Hospitalisations in previous year	none	–€100	none	–€100	2 days	+€150
Individual healthcare costs (= actuarial premium)	€250		€250		€1,000	
Net payment into RSCF: by person	–€250		–€250		+€500	
Net payment into RSCF: by insurer	–€250			+€250		

Risk structure compensation: 'Cherry-picking' of healthy clients is illegal in SHI systems, but, and perhaps more importantly, SHI systems also make cherry-picking economically pointless. This is done by a Risk Structure Compensation Fund (RSCF), which redistributes revenue from insurers with a disproportionate share of 'good risks' to insurers with a disproportionate share of 'bad risks'.

The purpose of the RSCF is to create a level playing field for insurers with very different patient populations, and, by extension, a level playing field for people with very different health statuses. After risk-adjustment payments from/into the RSCF, a person with complex chronic conditions is (*ex ante*) just as economically attractive to an insurer as a person in robust health.

A stylised example (although not too far away from how the Dutch RSCF really does work; see Schäfer et al. 2010: 81–83) of the mechanics of risk compensation is shown in Table 9. We assume that there are only three people, A, B and C, and two insurance companies, X and Y. A and B are the 'good risks': they are both 20 years old, have no chronic conditions, and no recent history of hospitalisation. C is the 'bad risk': 70 years old, suffering from thyroid disorder, and has been hospitalised in the previous year. Actuarial calculations show that average expected healthcare costs are €250 per year for somebody with the demographic and health profile of A or B, and €1,000 for somebody with C's profile. This is worked out by starting from a common baseline (namely average healthcare costs per capita), and then adding or deducting expected costs according to demographic and individual health risk factors. A picks Insurer X; B and C pick Insurer Y.

In a conventional insurance system, insurers would charge actuarial premiums: each individual's premium would be determined by their expected healthcare costs. A and B would pay €250 each, and C would pay €1,000.

Now suppose the government imposed community rating (coupled with an obligation to contract, because otherwise, insurers could simply reject the 'bad risk', Person C). Without risk structure compensation, this arrangement could not work. Insurer Y would have to hike Person B's premium in order to cross-subsidise Person C's, but then B would simply switch to Insurer X. The good risks would try to run away from the bad risk (because sharing an insurer with a bad risk makes their premiums go up), and the bad risk would try to run after the good risks (because sharing an insurer with good risks makes their premium go down). The result would be an endless cat-and-mouse game, a variation of the age-old problem of 'adverse selection'.

In principle, this problem could be solved by curtailing people's freedom to switch insurers, in order to maintain balanced risk pools, and/or by harmonising premiums across insurers. But this would weaken competition between insurers, and thus undermine the whole point of having a system of multiple insurers in the first place.

Table 10 Effect of Risk Structure Compensation Fund

	Person A	Person B	Person C	Total
Actuarial premiums (= conventional insurance system)	€250	€250	€1,000	€1,500
Community-rated premiums with risk structure compensation (= social health insurance system)	€500	€500	€500	€1,500
Net contribution to RSCF	€250	€250	−€500	€0

This is where the RSCF comes in. The RSCF would simply transfer €250 from Insurer X to Insurer Y – this is the amount required to compensate Insurer Y for the additional *per capita* costs that result from having signed on a bad risk, C. Insurers pass payments into/from the RSCF on to their clients, in the form of higher/lower premiums. Insurer X, the net contributor to the RSCF, has to raise its premiums, and Insurer Y, the net recipient from the RSCF, can cut its premiums. Both insurers would now charge a premium of €500 to all clients.

The transfer of €250 received by Y is really a *net* transfer. We could break it down into two steps: Insurer Y first pays €250 into the RSCF (for B, the good risk), and then receives a payment of €500 from the RSCF (for C, the bad risk). If Person B switches to Insurer X now, the transfer payment from Insurer X to Insurer Y would increase to €500. Both insurers would be as economically viable as they were before. This is the point of risk structure compensation: it does not matter who signs on the good risks and who signs on the bad risks.

This is because, ultimately, the RSCF does not redistribute between insurers, but between individuals. We can see this by simply comparing the premiums people would pay under actuarial conditions to the premiums they pay under community rating with risk structure compensation, as shown in Table 10. C receives an implicit subsidy of €500, paid jointly by A and B.

All five SHI countries run risk structure compensation schemes, but they differ in sophistication. Broadly speaking, the more closely RSCF payments match true cost differences between patient groups, the freer the insurance market can be. Under a hypothetical perfectly accurate RSCF system, differences in insurance premiums would be 100 per cent attributable to genuine differences in efficiency between insurers, and/or genuine differences in the cost of the services they offer. Competition would be of the 'good' kind ('who offers better services/is most efficiently run?'), not the 'bad' kind ('who is best at cherry-picking the easiest cases?'). But if RSCF payments vastly undercompensate for some patient groups and vastly overcompensate for others, some incentives for cherry-picking remain, and competition between insurers is distorted. Governments then need to interfere in the insurance market in other ways, such as by limiting free choice of insurer in order to maintain balanced risk pools. For example, in the German system, risk structure compensation only began in earnest in the early 1990s, and until then, movements between insurers were severely restricted (Breyer et al. 2005: 297–98; Oberender et al. 2002: 80).

The Belgian, German and Dutch RSC systems are probably the most sophisticated ones, the Israeli system the least, with the Swiss system also being fairly basic (van de Ven et al. 2013: 239–41).

It is clear that SHI systems are not pure market systems. The government mandates the purchase of a basic insurance package, defines what goes into that package, subsidises its purchase, obliges insurers to accept every applicant, bans actuarial premiums, and organises a complex redistribution scheme between insurers. On the other hand, though, people can freely choose between different insurers and different providers, which operate in a competitive marketplace.

The truth is that SHI systems are compatible with varying degrees of market orientation. We could imagine an SHI system in which the government severely restricts switching between health insurers, allows only one type of insurance contract, actively shapes and standardises the contractual relationships between insurers and providers, bans for-profit actors, and erects barriers to entry into and exit from the market. The Dutch system more or less fitted this description until the mid 2000s. But we could also imagine an SHI system in which the government limits its role in healthcare to the functions described in the preceding paragraph, and otherwise leaves the healthcare market to its own devices. Providers and insurers can freely enter and exit the market, they can freely integrate and demerge vertically and horizontally, they can offer a variety of insurance products, and there is great institutional plurality.

The five countries considered here are all somewhere in between, although we could not easily rank them from 'most market-oriented' to 'least market oriented'. They are all market driven in some respects, and state dominated in others, in ways that are difficult to trade off against one another. To give three examples:

- All systems ban the profit motive in some parts of the system, with no coherent pattern emerging. The Dutch system, for example, does not permit for-profit hospitals,[6] which the Swiss system is more relaxed about – but then, the Swiss system does not allow for-profit insurance, which the Dutch system is relaxed about. The health insurance market in the Netherlands happens to be dominated by non-profit actors (Schäfer et al. 2010: 31), but this is the result of historical legacies, not legal restrictions.
- Germany has one of the largest for-profit hospital sectors in the world, while the Dutch system has no for-profit

6 This does not mean that there is literally no single for-profit hospital in the Netherlands. It means that such a hospital must operate outside the statutory health system, like a private hospital in the UK.

hospitals. For hospital corporations such as Helios Kliniken, Rhön-Klinikum, Asklepios and Sana Kliniken, Germany is a multi-billion euro market, while the Netherlands is a no-go area. In this sense, the German hospital sector looks much more market-driven than its Dutch counterpart. And yet Germany operates a system of state hospital planning – covering private as well as public hospitals – in which politicians, not business owners or managers, decide where hospital capacity should be expanded and where it should be contracted. This system has no counterpart in the Netherlands, and to a Dutch hospital manager, it would probably look like Soviet-style central planning.

- SHI systems can offer 'meta-choice': people choose how much freedom of choice (of providers) they want to have. The default option is a health plan which offers unrestricted access to all health providers. At the opposite end of the spectrum is the 'HMO option', under which people completely waive their right of free provider choice, and limit themselves to an integrated multi-speciality health centre. Between these poles can be a broad spectrum of options, and greater restrictions come with greater premium discounts.

The Dutch system allows health plans which come with some minor restrictions on provider choice, but it does not offer anything approaching the HMO option. The Swiss system, somewhat oddly, allows both extremes, but nothing in between. Patients either have completely unrestricted provider choice (if they stick to the default option) or none (if they choose the HMO option).

So we cannot easily say whether one SHI system is more market-driven than another: it depends on which market freedoms we consider more important. What we can say, however, is that all of them are, in some ways, *more* market-oriented than the US system, which is generally perceived to be the Mecca of laissez-faire capitalism in healthcare. In the US system, almost a third of the population are covered by a government insurance programme, either Medicaid, Medicare or a military scheme (US Census Bureau 2013). They are thus taken out of the regular insurance market altogether (at least for primary insurance). Such parallel insurance systems do not exist in SHI systems. A long-term unemployed person in an SHI country could have the same health insurer as their employed neighbour, and if they become ill, they would go to the same doctor and to the same hospital. The only difference is that the long-term unemployed person would have their insurance premium paid by the government, while their employed neighbour would pay for it themselves. But there is no separate 'poor people's insurer' run by the government. Poor people participate in the regular insurance market just like everybody else.

Up to a point, SHI systems can be treated as a family and summarised together. The next sections will highlight a few notable features of individual systems that could be of relevance to the UK debate.

Notable features of the Dutch system

As mentioned, SHI systems are compatible with varying degrees of market orientation, and for most of its history, the Dutch system has been at the 'statist' end of the spectrum. This changed in the mid 2000s, when it moved a long way towards the opposite end.

The *Zorgverzekeringswet* (Health Insurance Act) of 2006 is often presented as the replacement of a state-centric, traditional 'Bismarckian' system with a new, more consumer-driven one, but this description can be misleading. There was never a 'big bang' in Dutch healthcare, and, for most people, nothing changed in 2006. What happened was that up until the mid 2000s, the contractual relationships between patients/policyholders, insurers and providers had been tightly regulated and standardised.

There were standard insurance contracts and there were nationwide collective agreements between representatives of all insurers on the one hand, and representatives of all providers on the other hand. Under those conditions, the point of having a system of competing multiple insurers becomes somewhat moot. It would be like a nationwide collective agreement between all retailers and all wholesalers: there might then still be a number of different supermarkets, but they would largely offer the same products at the same prices, with differentiation only happening at the margins.

In the mid 2000s, most of these constraints were removed. Insurers were allowed to negotiate individual agreements with selected providers, as well as integrate vertically with provider organisations. Switching insurers was also made easier and insurers were given greater scope for offering multiple insurance plans.

The reason why nothing special happened in 2006 or any other individual year was that the old collective agreements did not suddenly disappear. They remained in place as the default option, from which individual actors were now allowed to deviate, if they so chose.

One could compare this to 'Brexit', in the sense that nothing special will happen on the day when the UK formally ceases to be a member of the European Union. All the EU-derived legislation of the last four decades will still be in place, and the bulk of it will remain so for years and decades to come. What will change is that from then on, British legislation can diverge from this default option, if and when a deliberate decision to diverge from it is made.

In the same way, the Dutch health reforms were not an 'event'. There was no watershed moment that marked the end of the 'old system' and the beginning of a 'new system'. There was, at best, a moment after which individual system actors were given permission to deviate from a common baseline.

And even then, it was not a 'moment', but a process. As Schut and van de Ven (2011: 111) explain:

> [T]he supply side of the health-care market remained largely unchanged in 2006 and for the most part is still heavily regulated by the government. [...] [R]eform of the health insurance market represents only the first stage in the introduction of managed competition. The next stage, a complementary reform of the provider market, only began around 2006. Managed competition in Dutch healthcare therefore remains a work in progress.

For the reimbursement of hospitals, a free-pricing segment was created, within which individual insurers and individual providers could freely negotiate prices. Prices in this so-called 'Segment B' accounted for about a fifth of hospital revenue in 2008 (ibid.), a share which was then increased to about a third in 2011, and to over two thirds by subsequent reforms (OECD 2015: 248; Schut et al. 2013: 15–22). Costs in Segment B have so far increased at a slower rate than costs in Segment A (OECD 2015: 249), which could mean that insurers have been relatively successful at securing favourable deals on behalf of their policyholders, insofar as they have been given the remit. However, we cannot know whether free pricing is really the reason for the cost divergence, and either way, because of increases in demand, the cost of hospital care has still risen overall.

Health insurers have cut operating costs by about a tenth in the first years after the reform (Schut and van de Ven 2011: 114), and hospital productivity has also been growing at annual rates not far from 3 per cent (Mosca 2012; OECD 2015: 16). Again, however, a link with the market reforms would be difficult to prove, and hospital productivity growth had already begun to accelerate in the very early stages of reform.

What can be more easily attributed to the reforms is the fall in pharmaceutical costs. Schut and van de Ven (2011: 117) explain:

The individual bidding strategies had a dramatic effect on the prices of generics. List prices of the 10 biggest-selling generics fell by between 76% and 93% [...], leading to aggregate savings estimated at €348 million (69%) per year.

What has also been attributed to the reforms is the rapid decline in waiting times, once an endemic problem in the Netherlands. According to Siciliani et al. (2014: 300), this decline was the result of a change in payment systems, namely from block budgets to activity-based payments, combined with the expansion of selective contracting. Perhaps the best indication of success in this area is the fact that waiting times have dropped off the policy agenda: 'As a result of these reforms, waiting times are not a significant health policy issue as they were in the 1990s' (ibid.).

The Netherlands is one of the few countries for which data on waiting times is available in the same format as UK waiting times, which makes them directly comparable. As Figure 14 shows, with the exception of prostatectomy, average waiting times in the UK are between twice and almost three times as long as in the Netherlands.

What is much harder to assess is the reforms' impact on health outcomes and quality. We can see improvements in some time series data, both in absolute terms and relative to other countries. But we cannot assess to what extent these improvements can be attributed to recent reforms. What we do know is that (Schut and van de Ven 2011: 115–16):

Quality of care plays an increasing role in contracts between health insurers and hospitals. [...] [A]bout two-thirds [of hospitals] make agreements with health insurers about quality and almost 90% about reporting quality indicators [...] [S]ome health insurers also use outcome indicators when contracting selectively [...] The use of quality indicators for hospital care – especially those related to outcomes – is still in its infancy,

Figure 14 Average waiting times (number of days) for common surgical procedures, 2014 or latest available year: UK and Netherlands

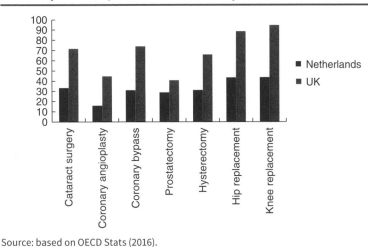

Source: based on OECD Stats (2016).

but health-care reform was an important catalyst for their development.

But, almost like the Commonwealth Fund study, this only tells us something about inputs and procedures. How successful insurers have been in these endeavours, and how those market-driven attempts to improve quality compare to earlier methods, is not clear.

Selective contracting has not yet had a transformative impact on healthcare delivery. It could only be truly effective if insurers could actively direct their policyholders towards providers with whom they maintain preferential contracts. So far, Dutch insurers have been very reluctant to try this, fearing that what would be perceived as meddling with patient choice would be punished by consumers (Schut and van de Ven 2011: 119).

The same holds for vertical integration. It would only make sense for insurers to take over provider organisations if they could direct their policyholders towards what would now be in-house facilities. This has proven difficult so far. There are various small-scale examples of vertical integration (Bijlsma et al. n.d.; Canoy and Sauter 2009), but only one of the large insurers has acquired its own primary care centres. Schut and van de Ven (2011: 119) explain:

> [T]he idea of health insurers interfering in medical practice remains a sensitive issue in the Netherlands [...] Health insurers are keen to avoid being seen as dictating to doctors which type of care they can prescribe to their patients.

It does not help that financial incentives are blunted in the Dutch system. Part of the insurance premium is hidden in a nominal 'employer contribution'. This means that if a policyholder accepted a low-cost health plan which placed limitations on provider choice, part of the cost savings would accrue to their employer, not the policyholder. The use of cost sharing is also very limited. Out-of-pocket spending accounts for an even smaller share of healthcare spending than in the UK (based on WHO 2015).

In short, a number of problems remain, and the market reforms have not always worked out as the Econ 101 textbook would predict. And yet, the Dutch system has improved in absolute and relative terms in a number of ways, and while a connection with the recent programme of market reforms cannot always be proven, it is at least plausible. A potential lesson for the UK is that even a radical health reform does not have to be disruptive. The reason why the Dutch reforms allowed continuity in healthcare delivery on the ground is *not* that the reforms were gradualist. Even if they had all been implemented in one day, they would still not have brought any revolutionary changes. This is because the reforms left the old arrangements in place as the default option, and simply gave individuals the freedom to diverge from this common baseline.

The Dutch example shows that a successful health system does not require the state to be actively involved in the provision of healthcare. The Dutch state does not own or run any hospitals, or, for that matter, insurers. It does not engage in hospital planning, and it does not subsidise any hospitals. The state sets the overall regulatory framework and ensures universal participation, but the rest is largely a matter between patients, insurers and providers. The delivery of healthcare in the Netherlands shows strong elements of a market discovery process.

Notable features of the Swiss system[7]

Cost sharing

Of all the SHI systems, the Swiss system offers the greatest freedom of choice between different insurance plans, and it also contains an interesting cost-sharing arrangement. As mentioned, in Switzerland, out-of-pocket payments by patients account for as much as a quarter of total healthcare spending (based on WHO 2015: 132–33), which is one of the highest shares in the developed world. And yet even according to the preferred study of NHS supporters, the Commonwealth Fund study, the Swiss system obtains the same score as the NHS in the 'Equity' category (Davis et al. 2014: 23–25).

The Swiss cost-sharing scheme has two main components: a deductible and proportional co-payments. The deductible is the minimum cost threshold beyond which insurance protection kicks in. In the default contract, it is set at CHF300 (≈£235) per annum, but people can voluntarily increase it to up to CHF2,500 (≈£1,950), in return for a premium rebate. Medical expenses

---

7   Unless otherwise indicated, the information in this section is based on European Observatory on Health Care Systems (2000), OECD (2006) and Daley and Gubb (2013).

below the deductible are not reimbursed by insurers, so up to that point, healthcare costs are fully paid out of pocket.

Insurers then reimburse 90 per cent of medical expenses above the deductible, leaving a 10 per cent co-payment for the patient. Co-payments, in turn, are capped at CHF700 (≈£550) per annum. Once a patient's cumulative medical bills have reached this ceiling, they incur no further expenses: from then on, their insurer pays for everything. Welfare recipients are exempt from co-payments, as are selected patient groups such as pregnant women (Leu et al. 2009: 21).

The cost-sharing scheme is illustrated in Figure 15, which shows the cumulative medical expenses that six hypothetical people incur throughout the year, and how those expenses are split between these people and their insurers.[8] All six are assumed to be on a standard contract, with an annual deductible of CHF300.

Person A only has minor ailments, leading to medical bills of no more than CHF300 for the whole year. Since this does not exceed the deductible, their insurance protection is not activated, so Person A has to pay all of their medical bills out of pocket. Person B is slightly less fortunate, incurring medical bills of CHF700. Out of this, they have to pay the deductible of CHF300, plus 10 per cent of the remaining CHF400. This means that Person B splits their medical bills roughly fifty–fifty with their insurer. Person C's medical bills sum up to CHF1,500, out of which they have to pay just over a quarter out of pocket, and Person D's add up to CHF5,000, out of which they pay about one seventh. Person E needs more extensive treatment, costing CHF8,000, but their out-of-pocket payments are not proportionately higher than those of Person D: this is because the protection of the co-payment cap has now kicked in. Person F incurs

---

8 We could also think of this as being one single person, requiring medical treatment six times a year, with the bars then showing their cumulative medical expenses.

Figure 15 How costs are shared in Switzerland: some hypothetical cases

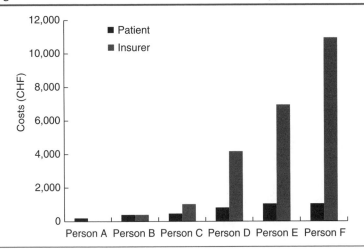

by far the highest medical expenses, but their out-of-pocket payments are no higher than Person E's. Since the co-payment cap has already been exceeded, out-of-pocket costs cannot rise any further. Beyond that threshold, all additional expenses are absorbed by the insurer.

The idea behind this system is simply that the purpose of health insurance is to protect people from *serious* financial risks associated with illness. This does not mean that *all* healthcare must be free at the point of use.

People can choose the level of their deductible. Increasing it from CHF300 to CHF1,000 would cut the insurance premium by just under one tenth, increasing it to CHF2,000 would cut it by about a fifth, and increasing it to CHF2,500 would cut the premium by a quarter.[9] Per capita healthcare expenditure of people on high-deductible plans is much smaller than those of people on standard contracts. There have been various attempts to estimate the extent

---

9   Author's calculation based on data from Comparis (2016).

to which the difference arises from self-selection (healthier people are more likely to choose high-deductible plans than people with health problems) and to what extent it is caused by differences in incentives (Werblow 2002; Schellhorn 2002a,b; Felder and Werblow 2003; Gerfin and Schellhorn 2005; Gardiol et al. 2005). Only the latter represents genuine cost savings; the former would persist even if everybody were forced into the minimum deductible plan. Estimates differ widely but it is safe to say that there is some effect over and above what can be explained by self-selection.

User charges are controversial in health economics. In theory, their impact could go either way, and the empirical evidence is mixed as well. Supporters argue that user charges discourage unnecessary demand and encourage cost-conscious behaviour (e.g. Drummond and Towse 2012; Kan and Suzuki 2010; Breyer et al. 2005: 263–67; Chiappori et al. 1998). Opponents argue that cost sharing unfairly penalises the poor and the sick, and that the only savings they achieve are of the false economy variety (Holst 2010). According to this argument, user charges deter people from seeking treatment in the early stages of an illness, when medical intervention would be most cost-effective. Instead, people put off treatment until the illness has reached a more advanced stage, when treatment is more complex and more expensive. User charges, in this view, lead to higher costs and worse health outcomes. Both supporters and opponents can point to case studies which support their point of view.

Much of the difference comes down to disagreements about the extent to which people have control over their healthcare costs. If we see them as largely fixed, the case for cost sharing is weak; if we see them as malleable, the case is stronger. By encouraging self-selection, the Swiss system of voluntary deductibles offers a potential way out of this conundrum. People who feel that they have little or no control over their healthcare costs will avoid high-deductible plans. Those plans will only be attractive to people who feel that they can indeed influence their healthcare costs. This means that the people are most *able* to respond to financial incentives will also be the ones who *face* the strongest financial incentives to economise on healthcare.

Meta-choice

In international overviews, health systems are sometimes classified by the extent to which patients enjoy free provider choice and/or direct access to specialists. The British and the Dutch systems, for example, are classified as gatekeeper systems, because patients cannot directly book an appointment with a specialist: they need to see their GP first and get a referral. The Austrian and the German systems, on the other hand, are not gatekeeper systems: specialist appointments are booked directly, without involving the GP.

It would be difficult to fit the Swiss system into either of those categories, because in Switzerland, these are not system-level decisions. They are individual decisions. People can choose health plans with and health plans without gatekeeping mechanisms; they can choose health plans with free provider choice and health plans without.

The default option is a health plan with unrestricted provider choice and without gatekeeping mechanisms. One alternative to this is the *Hausarztmodell*, a British-style gatekeeper model under which patients have to register with a GP and waive the right of direct access to specialist care. Another alternative is the *Telmedmodell*, which is also a gatekeeper model, under which patients must have a telephone consultation first before they can book any appointment. Both options typically come with premium reductions of between 15–20 per cent (Comparis 2016).

The most restrictive health plan, which reduces premiums by about a quarter compared to the standard plan, is the *HMO Modell*. Under this model, patients waive the right of free provider choice and restrict themselves to an integrated health centre.

In the UK, there has long been a debate about whether choice in healthcare is really desirable, and whether patients actually want choice. For example, writing for the *British Medical Journal*, Ellis (2013) argues:

> The language coming out of the NHS at the moment is all about choice. Well, choice is over-rated. [...] [T]he language of autonomy has been co-opted and corrupted by ideologues [...] as an excuse to bring in free market principles. [...] Patients don't want a thousand choices: they want a health service that will do right by them every time. And that is what we are in danger of losing.

To a Swiss observer, this debate must seem bizarre. In Switzerland, there would be no point in debating, in the abstract, whether 'patients' want choice. Patients choose how much choice they want. Those who do not value the right of free choice and/or direct access very much can waive some of those rights and cash in a premium discount.

Having said that, 'meta-choice' in the Swiss system is not an undistorted choice. Swiss hospitals are generously subsidised, which blunts incentives (van de Ven et al. 2013: 235; Breyer et al. 2005). Without subsidies, hospitals would have to charge insurers cost-covering prices. Health plans with free choice of hospital would then become relatively more expensive, and HMO plans would become relatively cheaper.

In summary, though, the Swiss system shows that even high degrees of cost sharing need not undermine access to healthcare, and that not everything that is commonly decided at the system level really must be decided at the system level.

Notable features of the German system

A historical idiosyncrasy of the German system is that it is split into two parallel health insurance systems. Nine out of ten people are covered by a 'run-of-the-mill' SHI system (called the GKV system), with community-rated premiums, a risk structure compensation fund, and all the rest. The remainder are covered by a conventional private health insurance system (called the PKV system[10]), with actuarial premiums and, consequently, no risk structure compensation.

This split is a historical anomaly, which goes all the way back to the 1880s, and which would be hard to justify if the system were set up today.[11] Nonetheless, the PKV pillar of the German system has developed an interesting feature which has lessons to offer to SHI systems as well: a system of accumulating old-age reserves.

We have seen in Chapter 2 that healthcare costs are flat for the first few decades of life, and then rise exponentially with age. Under an actuarial system, health insurance premiums would follow the same trajectory. Premiums would be cheap for young and middle-aged people, but, for the elderly, they would increase at an accelerating rate.

In order to prevent this, German PKV insurers are required to smooth premiums over people's lifetime. They do this by building up an old-age fund on behalf of their policyholders while they are of working age, and draw upon it in later years. In a stylised

---

10 GKV = *Gesetzliche Krankenversicherung,* 'statutory health insurance'; PKV = *Private Krankenversicherung,* 'private health insurance'.

11 The same split existed in the Dutch system until 2006. But then, the Dutch system was initially a replica of the German system, introduced under German occupation in 1944 as part of a longer-term plan to absorb the Netherlands into the envisaged *Großgermanisches Reich.* This meant that even the anomalies were copied.

Social insurance and conventional private insurance can sensibly coexist, if the former is used for statutory insurance, and the latter for voluntary supplementary insurance. But they get in each other's way when they are used as alternatives, as they are in Germany. By switching from the GKV system to the PKV system, the good risks can opt out of risk structure compensation, thus re-introducing the very problem of adverse selection that risk structure compensation was supposed to solve. Under some circumstances, people can even use the PKV system when they are healthy and their actuarial premium is low, and then switch back to the GKV system when they develop a serious medical condition, and their actuarial premium goes up.

Figure 16 Premium-smoothing: a hypothetical example

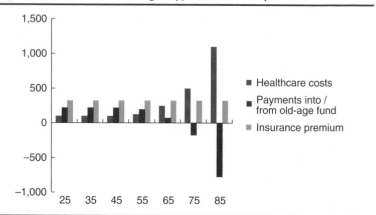

(yet not too unrealistic) form, Figure 16 illustrates how premium smoothing works.

The dark grey bars show an individual's healthcare costs over the lifecycle, the lighter bars show payments made into (and later: payments taken out of) the old-age fund by the insurer on behalf of that individual. The sum of the two is the insurance premium, which is held constant at 325 thalers per year throughout this individual's life. While that person is young, their insurance premiums greatly exceed their actual healthcare costs. The difference is paid into the old-age fund. At age 55, healthcare costs slowly begin to rise, but the premium is held constant, because payments into the old-age fund are decreased commensurately. At age 75, the person's healthcare costs exceed their insurance premium. The difference is settled by payments from the old-age fund. At age 85, healthcare costs have risen so much that insurance premiums can only cover a fraction. Deductions from the old-age fund are now no longer just a supplement, rather, they pay for the lion's share of this person's healthcare costs.

The old-age reserves held by all German PKV insurers taken together amount to about €170 billion, equivalent to around €20,000 per PKV policyholder. Annual additions to the fund account for about 5 per cent of the country's net savings rate (Schönfelder and Wild 2013: 28–29). Had the NHS built up the same amount of capital reserves per person, it could now have an old-age reserve fund of over £900 billion at its disposal.[12]

The system has its flaws. Premiums are not supposed to increase with age at all, but, in practice, they do, as insurers have persistently underestimated medical inflation. And old-age reserves are not portable between insurers, which means that above a certain age, switching insurers ceases to be a realistic option, as it would entail a loss of old-age reserves and a higher premium with the new insurer. This locks people into their insurance contracts and weakens competition between insurers.

Still, the German PKV system shows that health systems can run on a prefunded basis, just like pension systems. PAYGO-financed systems, whether for pensions or healthcare, are fair-weather systems. The PKV system is financially robust and sustainable. Its old-age fund represents a solid buffer, which leaves it well prepared not just for rainy days, but for demographic storms.

Notable features of the Israeli system

Opponents of pluralistic healthcare systems often argue that competition leads to fragmentation of services, and that the success of a health system depends, first and foremost, on its ability

---

12 This is an extremely crude back-of-the-envelope figure, which is only meant to give an idea of the order of magnitude. Demographic factors, medical input prices, the package of healthcare services and other relevant variables differ between the two countries, so one cannot simply extrapolate from the German figure in this way. But for the sake of the argument, if the NHS had built up old-age reserves averaging £15,000 per person, then for a UK population of 64.6 million, this would work out at £969 billion.

to deliver integrated care. A health system's actors, these critics argue, should cooperate, not compete; they should work *with* each other, not *against* each other. But this way of thinking completely misunderstands the nature and purpose of competition. Competition is *not* the opposite of cooperation, and it is *not* an obstacle to achieving integration of services. No health system demonstrates this more clearly than that of Israel.

The Israeli system is a system of competing integrated insurer–provider networks (Rosen et al. 2015). Israeli insurers directly employ physicians, and they own and run their own healthcare facilities. Most primary care and ambulatory specialist care is delivered in-house. The largest health insurer, Clalit, even runs its own hospitals – it is, in fact, one of the largest actors in the Israeli hospital sector.

There are also other forms of integration, which stop short of a merger of organisations. When Israeli insurers contract external providers, they often do not just passively reimburse costs, but try actively to shape the delivery of care (ibid.). Unlike most European insurers, Israeli insurers have the leverage to do so: they can channel their policyholders to contracted providers, which gives them the negotiating strength that comes with bulk-buying.

At least historically (this has changed in recent years), in European SHI systems, health insurance has been rather like car insurance: car insurers reimburse the cost of car repairs, but they would not get actively involved with coordinating car repair services, let alone run their own garages. The Israeli system, in contrast, is more like a system of competing gym chains, where members pay regular subscription fees and are, in return, entitled to use the in-house facilities.

In theory, the Swiss and the Dutch systems (but not, currently, the Belgian or the German systems) could also evolve in the Israeli direction. In Switzerland, this would happen if people started to sign up for HMO health plans in much greater numbers, and if insurers responded by expanding that option. In the Netherlands, this would happen if people began to switch to those insurers that are most proactive in terms of vertical integration, and became generally less resistant to being channelled to contracted providers.

Either way, it becomes clear that 'marketisation' must *not* be seen as the opposite of integration. A market is an overall framework in which integrated models compete with specialised models. Competition can even be a catalyst for integration, if competitive pressures force providers to cooperate more closely across disciplinary boundaries than they otherwise would, in order to exploit economies of scope.

Conclusion

There is a tendency in the UK to eulogise the National Health Service for minor achievements, and this is partly because the NHS is held to unrealistically low standards. NHS care is either compared to American healthcare, or to healthcare as it was prior to 1948, or simply to a system without any form of insurance. SHI systems offer a more realistic benchmark. Like the NHS, SHI systems also achieve universal and equitable access to healthcare, and they consistently outperform the NHS on measures of health outcomes and quality. The UK is better at keeping spending under control, but as explained in Chapter 2, this must not be confused with superior efficiency.

The Dutch example shows that a successful healthcare system needs neither state-owned/run hospitals, nor state hospital planning, nor hospital subsidies. The Swiss example shows that cost-sharing need not undermine equity, and that matters which we would normally think of as political decisions can be turned into individual decisions. The German PKV pillar shows that healthcare can be prefunded, just like a pension system. The Israeli system shows how competition and integration can be compatible.

Taken together, these examples show that by looking inwards, and pretending that the only conceivable alternative to the NHS is the American system, we are missing out on interesting developments and valuable lessons from elsewhere.

5 TOWARDS A PLURALISTIC, SUSTAINABLE HEALTHCARE SYSTEM: A STRATEGY FOR AN ORDERLY TRANSITION

The 'alternative history' section in Chapter 1 sketched out a hypothetical consumer-centred, market-based system that could have developed if the NHS had never been created. Chapter 4 gave an overview of health systems that really have, in some respects, evolved along those lines. None of these systems could be considered a real-world proxy for the hypothetical system described in the opening chapter, but most of the individual elements described there have a real-world equivalent somewhere, even if they are not all in one place.

Chapter 3 showed how the quasi-market reforms have already converted the NHS into a system in which patients can choose providers and in which funding follows patients, and that this can be considered a success story as far as it goes.

This chapter will tie up the loose ends, and show how the quasi-market reforms of the 2000s can be built upon in order to move towards a consumer-centric system.

The quasi-market: finishing the job

Completing provider choice reform

On paper, patients have been enjoying free choice of provider at the point of referral since 2008. In reality, most GPs simply continue to refer patients as they see fit. According to patient surveys, only about one in three patients is being offered a choice of provider upon referral (Ham et al. 2015: 51). If anything, this proportion has recently been falling, not rising, so it cannot just be explained by the fact that patient choice is still relatively novel.

A solution could be to change referral practices more thoroughly. GPs should not have an automatic right to refer patients to any specific provider. Rather, a letter of referral should simply be a voucher that patients can redeem at any provider offering the relevant service, just like a prescription can be used at any pharmacy offering the relevant drug.

Of course, GPs could still advise their patients and recommend specific providers, and they could still refer patients if a patient specifically instructs them to do so. Also, as described in Chapter 4, 'free choice' does not have to mean that any patient can choose any provider in the country. There can be good reasons for setting up managed care networks with pre-established referral patterns, and arrangements under which patients voluntarily waive some of their freedom of provider choice. But the default option should be the 'voucher model' and unrestricted choice of any willing provider. Everything else would be models that a patient has to deliberately opt into.

As described in Chapter 3, the empirical evidence on patient choice has been positive. Patient choice fuels competition, which increases provider performance and productivity. This does not mean that the same benefits can be reaped all over again if patient choice is expanded further. But there is no reason to stop at the current halfway house.

Completing the conversion into Foundation Trusts

All hospital trusts should be converted into free-standing Foundation Trusts. This was originally the intention when Foundation Trust status was created, and this policy aim has never been officially abandoned, either by the coalition or the Conservative majority government. The reform just stalled, presumably because other developments – the 2012 Health and Social Care Act, the failure to meet important waiting time targets, and, later, the conflicts around the junior doctors' strike – have taken up most of the political energy. And yet, Foundation Trust status, and the greater independence that comes with it, is a logical correlate of the change in payment systems and the introduction of patient choice.

Completing the rollout of activity-based payments

In the mid 2000s, the Labour government phased in the Payment by Results (PbR) system, alongside other formulas which pay providers by activity levels. And yet, at the time of writing, the vast majority of hospital trusts in the country are in deficit, demonstrating that providers could not realistically sustain themselves on the basis of PbR tariffs alone. This limits the effectiveness of the PbR system. While PbR is often described as a system in which 'the money follows the patient', it would be more accurate to describe it as one in which 'some money follows some patients'. It is already the case that 'many [providers] have effectively become dependent on the Department of Health for financial support' (Ham et al. 2015: 37), and this is set to accelerate. Eventually, the deficits will have to be settled by *ad hoc* bailouts and other politically determined transfers.

This stands in contrast with the Dutch system, where hospitals are expected to be fully self-sustaining, partly on the basis of PbR-like payments, and partly on the basis of contracts negotiated with individual health insurers. They do not receive government subsidies (van de Ven et al. 2013: 235). This is also true of the Israeli SHI system.

To increase the payment system's effectiveness, the reach of activity-based payments should be extended, and the tariffs should be set in such a way that the vast majority of providers can be fully self-sustaining on the basis of tariff revenue alone. Other payments would be phased out. This would probably necessitate a greater differentiation of tariffs by case severity: providers should not be penalised for treating especially complicated cases, or tempted to cherry-pick the relatively easy cases.

If activity-based payments became the sole source of provider revenue, healthcare funding would, in effect, be allocated by patients, not politicians or civil servants. Patients would allocate funding – not via the ballot box, by voting (very indirectly) for a particular health policy platform, but simply via the individual choices they make when seeking treatment. Since the money would now truly follow the patient, any decision to switch from provider X to provider Y, or from treatment A to treatment B, would automatically lead to a reallocation of resources within the health sector.

Standardised activity-based formulas make providers responsive to patient demand, while also rewarding efficiency. Under such a formula, providers gain by attracting more patients, treating them in a cost-effective manner, and speeding up their recovery.

Free entry and exit

Crucially, this change in the funding method would have to be coupled with a no-bailout clause. If a provider fails to attract enough patients to survive economically, it should not survive economically. Bankruptcies and takeovers of failing providers by better-performing ones would then become a normal occurrence.

In the Dutch system, the absence of a no-bailout clause was initially a critical omission in the transition to a more market-oriented provider sector, and a number of failing providers were bailed out in various ways (Kocsis et al. 2012). More recently, however, the government declared its intention not to intervene prior to a bankruptcy any more. Whether this declaration is credible remains to be seen, but when a large hospital near Rotterdam failed in 2013, the government did not come to its rescue. (The hospital in question was immediately taken over by three other ones.)

Takeovers of this kind, and even closures, occur in the UK as well (see Ham et al. 2015: 13–15), but they occur on an *ad hoc* basis. They are not hardwired into the system. A broadening of activity-based payment, coupled with a no-bailout clause and, potentially, a clarification of the legal framework for orderly defaults and takeovers, would rectify this situation.

One reason why the Dutch no-bailout clause might not be sustainable in the long term is the ban on for-profit providers in the Dutch hospital sector: there might not always be a suitable non-profit organisation standing ready to take over a failing provider. As Kocsis et al. (2012: 18–19) explain:

> With hospitals liquidating, there should also be room for new entrants. As the NFP [not for profit] constraint hinders the possibilities to attract new capital, there is more pressure on the government as a third party to bail hospitals out.

In trying to 'dynamise' the provider sector, the UK should therefore not replicate the Dutch ban on for-profit actors. The system should be neutral with regard to ownership structure and legal form.

Note that this suggestion is *not* predicated on a belief that for-profit actors are somehow inherently more efficient, or more innovative, than other actors. There is nothing special about the profit motive. The argument here is simply that a ban on for-profit actors unnecessarily narrows the pool of potential entrants. It is a market entry barrier, which weakens competition and blocks access to capital.

Private providers should, however, face the same obligations as NHS trusts. They should also be obliged to collate and publish clinical outcome data, such as standardised mortality rates, in a format which makes their performance comparable with that of NHS providers. They should not receive any subsidies or other forms of government support. They should not be allowed to free-ride on the NHS. Whenever they fall back on NHS providers, they should pay in full for any benefits received.

Note that people who distrust for-profit actors, or who see for-profit healthcare as morally wrong regardless of the outcomes it produces, would still be free to avoid those actors. In this respect, NHS 'purists', who argue that for-profit actors should not be allowed to provide publicly funded healthcare on the grounds that 'the people' do not want their healthcare to be provided for a profit, are contradicting themselves. Surely, if 'the people' truly share those anti-profit convictions, and act upon them, the for-profit sector will always be at best a fringe phenomenon. There would then be no need to specifically exclude for-profit providers or put up barriers against them. They would simply not be viable, for the same reason that a steak house would not be viable in a neighbourhood dominated by vegans and vegetarians.

The reason, of course, why NHS purists want to ban for-profit actors is that 'the people' do not universally share their views. The British Social Attitudes Survey (BSA) asks people whether they would prefer treatment from an NHS provider, a private for-profit or a private non-profit provider if given the choice. As noted in Chapter 1, 43 per cent express no general preference for either sector, and a further 18 per cent express an active preference for the independent sector. Among people born after 1979, only about a third have a general preference for NHS providers. These are remarkable results given the direction of 'social desirability bias': there might be some respondents who are really indifferent, but who feel socially obliged to express a preference for the NHS. But there are surely no respondents who feel socially obliged to hide their pro-NHS preference. So it becomes clear that if these surveys are even loosely correlated to how people would actually behave, there is room for a large independent health sector in the UK. Under those circumstances, the only way to make the NHS conform to the purist vision is to make sure that patients are never given a choice, to prevent them from making 'impure' choices. Purists need to impose their personal preferences on everybody else, because most people do not share those preferences and would not abide by them voluntarily.

The idea of letting providers fail would definitely be politically controversial in the UK. Reform supporters must therefore emphasise that this coin has a flipside: a system that prevents market exits also prevents market entries. If underperforming providers are never allowed to fail, then better-performing ones will never be given room to expand, and potentially successful newcomers will never be given a chance even to get off the ground. A system that does not allow failure is like a blocked drainpipe, which does not let in any fresh water because the standing water cannot flow off.

Unblocking the drainpipe would not have any immediate effects. The health sector is not like, say, the restaurant sector, where entries and exits happen on a daily basis. It is a sector characterised by (a quite rational) inertia and path-dependency. But it is a way to improve the sector's dynamic efficiency.

Free choice of Clinical Commissioning Group

Since the mid 2000s, there have been significant attempts to promote patient choice and competition in the sphere of provision, but there have been no attempts at all to allow competition on the commissioning side. The idea that patients should be allocated to hospitals purely on the basis of geography has rightly been abandoned as anachronistic, but patients are still allocated to commissioners (and to a lesser extent, GPs) on precisely that basis. Patients can access information about the performance of providers, but not about the performance of commissioners. The entry of Independent Sector Treatment Centres has been actively promoted, but the existence of 'independent sector commissioners' has never even been considered. Healthcare commissioners remain local monopolies. Perhaps unsurprisingly, then, evaluations of the effectiveness of healthcare commissioning in the UK tend to be lukewarm (Smith and Curry 2011; Ham et al. 2011). This is what we should expect if relatively successful commissioners cannot expand, and if unsuccessful ones cannot shrink or disappear.

According to Higgins (2007: 23), it is:

> [o]ne of the most puzzling aspects of [...] commissioning arrangements [...] that commissioners must be defined by geography and by resident population. Commissioners in other countries can be organised around communities of interest [...] but there is no automatic assumption that they would serve a geographical catchment area. [...]
>
> There is no reason [...] why a commissioner based in Hastings could not purchase services in Halifax for a subscriber who lived there. [...] Many patients may continue to prefer to receive their care close to home, but that is different from arguing that their commissioner should be based locally too.

The link between commissioning and geography should be severed. People should be free to register directly (not via their GP) with any Clinical Commissioning Group they see fit, wherever they are based, and wherever the CCG may be based. This would create competition between CCGs, and it would complement the quasi-market on the provider side with a quasi-market on the commissioner side. Commissioning activities would no longer be shaped by politically determined geographical boundaries. CCGs would be able to negotiate and contract with providers up and down the country, or, for that matter, internationally.

In the short term, this would have no noticeable effect. CCGs may have roles that are vaguely comparable to those of insurers in SHI systems, but the huge difference is that in SHI systems, insurers, or at least the larger ones, are household names with distinct brand identities. In Switzerland, 'Helsana', 'Swica', 'Visana', etc., are brand names that the proverbial man in the street would recognise, as are 'Techniker Krankenkasse', 'Barmer GEK' or 'DAK-Gesundheit' in Germany. One could not say the same about 'NHS Milton Keynes CCG' or 'NHS Mid Essex CCG' in the UK.

So giving people the opportunity to switch CCGs is not enough. CCGs must also be given the freedom to develop their own profiles and specialities, and build up brand recognition. They should also be free to merge and demerge with other CCGs, so that their 'optimal' size and scope could be discovered through a competitive process, as opposed to political or bureaucratic fiat.

Two preconditions would have to be fulfilled first. Firstly, the budgets of CCGs would have to correspond much more closely to the health risk profiles of the populations they cover. Allocating budgets on the basis of risk profiles would create an implicit risk structure compensation mechanism, not unlike the RSCFs in SHI systems.

Unlike the latter, this would, however, be a 'virtual RSCF'. The German *Risikostrukturausgleich*, for example, is an actual institution (more precisely, a division within the Department of Health), with offices and people working there. This institution would not be replicated in the UK. The existing organisational structures would be maintained, but within them, the methods of allocating budgets would become more fine-grained. For the actuarial calculations, a template from an SHI system could be used as the starting point.

The second precondition is the specification of an explicit minimum 'healthcare basket', a set list of medical products and services which all CCGs have to offer. In SHI systems, this is standard practice (van de Ven et al. 2013: 230). A Belgian or a

Dutch patient could easily find out whether or not they are entitled to, for example, a particular drug. A British patient could not so easily do this, because on the NHS, such matters are handled in a much more discretionary manner.

However, since the end of the 1990s, there have been some steps towards formalising this process and reducing discretion (see Mason 2005). From here, it should be a relatively small step towards explicitly defining a minimum healthcare basket. CCGs would be free to offer additional services on top.

The freedom to opt out of NHS commissioning

Once these two preconditions have been met – an implicit risk structure compensation scheme is up and running, and a minimum healthcare basket has been specified – there is no reason why the commissioning/insurance side should not be opened to non-NHS actors, for-profit or non-profit. Among the latter, obvious candidates would be patient groups, a possibility explored by Howes (2013), who describes a system in which 'Patient-led Commissioning Groups' (PCGs) operate alongside CCGs. Other obvious candidates are health insurance companies and integrated healthcare groups. Trade unions, professional associations and large employers would also be able to set up their own schemes. So would individual GP surgeries, if some of them wanted to revert to something akin to the 1990s model of GP fundholding.

When people opt into these non-NHS commissioning/insurance groups, the latter would be allocated the same risk-adjusted budget that a CCG would receive. Just as the money follows the patient when they choose providers, it would now also follow them when they choose commissioners/insurers. There should be no attempt to specifically 'promote' or 'encourage' non-NHS commissioners/insurers; they should simply have the same rights and the same obligations as CCGs.

While this arrangement could massively increase the size of the private healthcare market, it would, in important ways, be *less* lucrative to the private sector's incumbents than the status quo. At the moment, private healthcare companies sometimes offer their clients cash payments if they seek treatment from the NHS rather than from the company's own in-house providers. Clive Peedell of the National Health Action Party (NHA) describes this practice as:

> an outrageous example of how the private healthcare sector is happy to take patients' money but then turns to the NHS when it realises it can't afford to meet the cost of treating patients privately. It looks like Bupa calculated that it's cheaper for them to pay patients to use the NHS than fork out themselves for private treatment.[1]

Such 'cherry-picking' could not happen under the arrangement proposed here. Private healthcare groups would have to cover the same minimum healthcare basket that an NHS-CCG would cover. They could, of course, outsource services to NHS providers if they find this cheaper than providing them in-house, or if they lack the relevant in-house expertise. But they would then have to pay the cost of that service in full, or, more precisely, they would have to pay the same regular tariff that an NHS-CCG would pay.

Mergers and takeovers between CCGs and non-CCG commissioners/insurers should also be permitted (subject to competition law), and a legal framework for an orderly default of a CCG would have to be created.

It would take a while to get these new independent sector commissioner-insurers off the ground, and even the already well-established private healthcare groups would not immediately

1 Bupa's £2,000 'bribes' for members to use the NHS: Campaigners say medical insurer dumps patients on health service because procedures they need are most expensive. *Daily Mail*, 10 April 2014.

stand ready to make much of the new opportunities that this would present them with. Private healthcare in the UK is currently oriented towards a luxury segment. It is not set up to have mass market appeal. One could almost compare it to the state of the airline industry prior to deregulation, when the likes of British Airways, American Airlines and Lufthansa shared a relatively small market, consisting mainly of fairly affluent customers, between them. The health sector equivalents of EasyJet, Ryanair and Norwegian have not even been founded yet (or if they have, they have stayed under the radar so far). So if a 'quick fix' exists, this would not be it.

Vertical and horizontal integration

Subject to competition law, CCGs and other commissioning/insurance organisations should be free to experiment with various forms of vertical and horizontal integration and demerging. This would give rise to a market discovery process in which different organisational models can be tried and tested against each other. As in the Netherlands, this could involve insurers running their own pharmacies and/or primary care centres, or acquiring minority stakes in them. As in Israel and, to a lesser extent, Switzerland, this could involve the fully integrated insurer/provider organisation, a one-stop-shop which runs its own hospitals, multi-speciality clinics, primary care centres, and which also provides insurance functions.

We cannot work out on a blackboard what the 'optimal' structure of healthcare delivery is. We cannot know in advance which aspects of healthcare are best bundled within a single organisation, which are best split and carried out by organisations that specialise in them, and when it makes most sense to share tasks between organisations that are independent but closely coordinated. This depends on a myriad of factors that are in constant flux, such as transaction costs, the ability to judge the quality of outcomes, the need for flexibility, the degree to which objectives and incentives are aligned, organisational and professional cultures, and so on.

In any health system, regardless of whether it is state run, market based, corporatist, or something else, there are competing visions of how healthcare ought to be delivered. In the current system, this manifests itself in a constant drive towards reorganisation. Bevan et al. (2014: 29) speak of an:

> appetite of successive secretaries of state for structural reorganisation [...] Timmins rightly observes that this has reached the point at which 'organisation, re-organisation and re-disorganisation' almost might be dubbed the English NHS 'disease'.

The reforms proposed here would mean the end of political reorganisation and the beginning of reorganisation by the market. Nobody would have the power to impose a reorganisation from above and change healthcare delivery patterns across the country as a whole. Rather, different actors would do things differently, and in this way, they would learn what works and what does not. Successful models of delivery would be imitated by others and spread, unsuccessful ones would be modified.

Freedom of choice over the depth and scope of coverage

As mentioned in Chapter 4, the empirical evidence on the effectiveness of cost-sharing schemes is very mixed. This is not too surprising: cost-sharing schemes come in all shapes and sizes, and we would expect some of them to work and others not. There is therefore a case for having various competing cost-sharing schemes, as opposed to a single one devised in Whitehall. Like almost everything in the system proposed here, cost sharing would be subject to a trial-and-error process.

In the UK, there is a very strong social consensus around the principle that healthcare should be free at the point of use, and it is unlikely that there will ever be popular support for a general change to this status. But this does not preclude a system of *voluntary* user charges, which people can opt into.

The Swiss system, which has been described in the previous chapter, is instructive in this regard. In Switzerland, the default option for health insurance is a low-deductible policy. But people have the option to voluntarily increase this deductible, and those who do so receive a premium rebate from their insurer. Some patients therefore pay substantial amounts out of pocket – but only if they have made an active choice to opt out of the standard contract and into a high-deductible plan. Nobody is forced to do so, and people can always go back to the low-deductible plan in the next contract period.

Voluntary deductibles exploit the advantages of cost-sharing arrangements while avoiding the risks. The system encourages self-selection, with healthier patients choosing higher deductibles. Thus, the people who have least control over their healthcare consumption – for example, the long-term sick – are still fully protected, while those with the highest degree of control over their healthcare consumption will also face the strongest incentives to economise.

The UK could adopt a variant of this system of voluntarily user charges. Unlike in the Swiss system, the default option would have to be a plan in which healthcare is completely free at the point of use. But CCGs and other financing agents should be allowed to offer alternative plans with user charges, and offer cash payments to people who choose those plans.

The Swiss system, though, is far from perfect, and should not be directly copied. In Switzerland, people can vary the level of the deductible, but not the structure of user charges, which limits the scope to experiment with various incentives structures. Swiss insurers could not, for example, vary the co-payment rate, which is a fixed 10 per cent. Nor could they offer a so-called 'doughnut hole plan', which is similar to a deductible, except that it starts at a higher level of spending.

Under a standard deductible of, say, £500, costs of up to £500 are paid by the patient, while costs above £500 are paid by the insurer. If the rebate for accepting that deductible is, say, £100, then that plan will only be attractive to people who have a realistic chance to keep their medical bills below £100. But people with chronic conditions, who do not have that chance, might still be able to influence their healthcare costs.

Suppose a diabetic knows that their medical spending usually exceeds £1,000, but they also know that if they make certain changes to their lifestyle and monitor their condition carefully, they can keep spending below that level. For that person, it could make sense to adopt a doughnut hole plan in which the first £1,000 of medical costs are covered by their insurer, while all spending above £1,500 is also covered, but spending between £1,000 and £1,500 falls on the patient. This is like a £500 deductible that has been shifted upwards.

The UK should adopt a flexible system in which cost-sharing schemes with completely different incentive structures can be tried and tested. The only restriction would be an absolute annual cap on the sum of individual user payments, regardless of the composition of those payments. In Switzerland, the maximum deductible is CHF2,500, and co-payments are capped at CHF700, which means that the absolute maximum that a Swiss patient could ever pay in a year is CHF3,200 (≈£2,500).[2] An overall cap of this type should be adopted in the UK as well.

Insurers should also be allowed to offer health plans which come with gatekeeping mechanisms and/or limitations on provider choice, comparable to the Swiss *Telmedmodell* and the *HMO Modell* (outlined in Chapter 4).

---

2   In Switzerland, only about 4 per cent of the population choose the maximum deductible plan (Felder and Werblow 2003: 44).

The status quo would remain the default option, and for people who are happy with current arrangements, nothing would change. But insurers would be able to offer alternative plans for people who are prepared to accept greater financial responsibility for their healthcare costs and/or some restrictions on provider choice, in return for a cash payment. Insurers would face strong incentives to devise these schemes in such a way that they result in genuine cost savings. If the cash payments they have to offer in order to entice people into a particular health plan exceed the cost savings resulting from that plan, the insurer would lose money. It would then be in their own interest to modify the loss-making health plan, or discontinue it. Critics believe that cost-sharing schemes only lead to false economy savings: people are deterred from seeking treatment in the early stages of an illness and procrastinate until the illness has progressed to a more serious stage. Under the proposal described here, it would be in the insurer's best interest to avoid this. If small savings today lead to large costs tomorrow, then under our proposal, the bulk of these costs would fall upon the insurer.

Prefunding healthcare costs

As with pensions, the only root-and-branch solution to demographic challenges would be to move from a PAYGO-system to a prefunded one. Insurers would build up a capital stock for their members while they are young, and draw on it when their members reach old age. The case for prefunding healthcare is theoretically well established, and there are various proposals for how the transition to a fully or partially prefunded model could work. Feldstein develops a proposal for prefunding Medicare, the US government insurance programme for the retired. Stabile and Greenblatt (2010) explain how Pharmacare, a Canadian insurance programme covering the cost of pharmaceuticals, could be changed to a prefunded basis. The federal government of Canada also runs a programme of transfers to assist regional governments with the healthcare costs of the elderly. Robson (2002) outlines a proposal for prefunding this federal programme. Felder (2003) comes up with an innovative plan, under which Germany's Risk Structure Compensation Fund, the *Risikostrukturausgleich*, would simultaneously become an old-age reserve fund.

There are also examples of such transitions for pension systems (e.g. Niemietz 2007), and we can draw inferences from these experiences. The transition could work like this: CCGs and non-NHS insurers would be required to start building up old-age reserves for every member below a certain age. Each of these members would then have an old-age fund allocated to them, held by their CCG/insurer.

For those close to retirement age or above, it is too late to build up reserves, so for them, healthcare should continue to be financed on a PAYGO basis. There should be no changes for this group.

Most people will fall somewhere in between: there will still be time to build up *some* reserves for them, but not enough fully to cover their old-age healthcare costs. For them, CCGs/insurers should still set up old-age accounts, and the state should fill the accounts with government bonds in order to make up for the 'missing' reserves. This does not entail an increase in government debt; it merely entails a conversion of implicit into explicit debt. The current system contains an implicit promise to those of working age that when they reach old age, they will be entitled to (at least) the same standard of healthcare that the older generation currently enjoys. That promise has a monetary value, and the transition to a funded system would force the government to put a number on it.

During the transition, there would be a cash-flow deficit, as the young generation would have to put aside the funds to meet their own future healthcare costs, while still having to pay for the healthcare costs of the elderly. This transitional cost would have to be spread over several generations (Booth and Niemietz 2015). But there would also be a partial self-financing effect. In Chile, which began the transition from a PAYGO pension system to a prefunded one in 1981, the conversion of an implicit debt into an explicit one encouraged a political culture of fiscal prudence. Spending reductions and large-scale privatisations that might not otherwise have been politically feasible became feasible (Niemietz 2007).

Unlike under a system of individual medical savings accounts (as in Singapore), the method of prefunding suggested here would not reduce the extent of risk sharing in healthcare financing. People in good health would still cross-subsidise people in poor health. But there would be no systematic intergenerational redistribution. Today's young people would not expect an as yet unborn future generation to pay for their future healthcare costs. They would make provisions for their old age in due time.

Unlike in the German PKV system, members' old-age reserves should be fully portable between CCGs/insurers, so that people can switch CCGs/insurers at any time, even at an advanced age. Also, unlike German PKV insurers, all British CCGs/insurers would be part of the same (virtual) risk structure compensation scheme. Thus, the prefunding scheme proposed here would not be a copy of the German PKV system, which should be seen as a historical special case rather than a 'model' one would emulate. The actuarial calculations of German PKV insurers, however, could be used as a template.

Selective contracting

Fixed national tariffs would remain the default option for reimbursing providers. But insurers and providers could be given the freedom to deviate from this baseline and negotiate their own alternative arrangements. In the past, the problem with such selective contracting agreements was that they quickly led to price competition, and price competition cannot work effectively when quality cannot be adequately measured and monitored. But the availability of clinical data has greatly improved since the 1990s, when selective contracting was last tried, and as it continues to improve further, insurers and providers can be given greater freedoms to devise their own contractual arrangements.

The effects of different payment structures have been amply researched (Charlesworth et al. 2012), and that research has rarely come up with anything conclusive. We simply do not know what is the best way to reimburse providers; we do not know how to design a payment system that aligns incentives. The best we can hope for is a trial-and-error process that gradually brings us a bit closer to a workable solution.

Conclusion

The proposals in this chapter have not been plucked out of thin air. They are informed by solid evidence of what has worked in the recent past and of what has worked in some of the world's best healthcare systems. They do not amount to a plan for a revolution, and this is not because they are, in themselves, 'gradualist': even if all the proposals outlined here were implemented in a single day and with immediate effect, nothing would be different on the day after. The old structures and arrangements would still be in place, unchanged, in the same way in which EU-derived legislation will still be in place after Brexit, and not an aspect of it will change until somebody takes an active decision to change it.

From then on, however, the health system's actors would be free to deviate from this common baseline and make alternative arrangements. Patients would be free to switch to other CCGs or non-NHS commissioner-insurers, or, indeed, to get together with like-minded people and set up completely new commissioning/insurance organisations of their own. Healthcare purchasers, meanwhile, would be free to negotiate alternative arrangements with selected healthcare providers, if all sides involved agreed to do so. This could mean vertical integration, it could mean the establishment of 'managed care' groups, or it could mean experimenting with different payment formulas, such as a scheme of performance-related pay. They would also be free to devise alternative health plans, which patients could voluntarily opt into. These could include plans with voluntary cost-sharing arrangements, or plans which direct patients to a preselected panel of providers. Apart from that, the main pillars of the quasi-market – patient choice, money follows patients, self-governing providers – would be strengthened, and the weak incentives contained in them would be turned into high-powered incentives.

An agenda for revolutionary change is neither necessary – the current quasi-market is not the worst place to start from – nor desirable. System-level characteristics, such as whether a system is a single-payer or a multi-payer system, or whether it is funded from taxation or insurance premiums, are of great interest to health economists. But the people who actually make a system work on the ground, will not, on a day-to-day basis, think of it in such abstract terms. They will think of it as a local network of relationships between patients, family doctors, specialists, nurses and other stakeholders. A leitmotiv of the proposals outlined above is the avoidance of unnecessary disruptions to those relationships: reformers should seek to leave these people alone and let them get on with their work.

The NHS has a totemic status, but NHS 'purism' is a giant with clay feet. It rests on two critical assumptions, namely that the only conceivable alternative to the NHS is the American system and that only a nationalised system can guarantee access to healthcare irrespective of ability to pay. These assumptions are never explicitly spelt out, because if they were, their absurdity would immediately become apparent.

They have nonetheless dominated the debate for a long time. Reminiscing about the healthcare debates of the 1960s and early 1970s, Klein (2003: 176) explains:

> [Richard Titmuss] was emphatic in his rejection of consumer choice in health care [...]
>
> Titmuss' apparent rejection of choice [...] was made in the course of his battle with the Institute of Economic Affairs (IEA), which in the 1960s was the lonely flag-carrier for private markets in healthcare and other social services. For Titmuss this raised the spectre of American-style health care – and he devoted much energy to expounding the inadequacies of the US system. [...]
>
> It was, in a sense, too easy: it encouraged a certain degree of chauvinistic complacency about Britain's NHS which might have been dispelled by comparing the UK with, say, Sweden and France. [...]
>
> [B]y using the United States case as a stick to beat the IEA [...] Titmuss left a legacy of suspicion in the social policy community towards anything which might be described (often wrongly) as the adoption of American-style ideas or policies. To use a vocabulary of competition, choice and markets was for long guaranteed to produce a knee-jerk reaction of indignation.

In this sense, nothing much has changed in half a century. And yet, the quasi-market reforms have let the genie out of the bottle; and while avoiding international comparisons was easy when the health sector accounted for no more than one twentieth of GDP, it may not remain so easy for much longer, now that it accounts for about twice that share.

Would the proposals developed here spell the end of the NHS? Ultimately, yes. Over time, the health sector would become so pluralistic and polycentric that one could no longer think of it as a single 'service', let alone a 'national' one. The 'N' and the 'S' in

'NHS' would fade and ultimately disappear, but the 'H' would gain at their expense. The UK would lose a beloved national symbol, but it would also gain something in the process: a health system that actually delivers.

REFERENCES

Allemani, C., Weir, H., Carreira, H., Harewood, R., Spika, D., Wang, X., Bannon, F., Ahn, J., Johnson, C., Bonaventure, A., Marcos-Gragera, R., Stiller, C., Azevedo e Silva, G., Chen, W., Ogunbiyi, O., Rachet, B., Soeberg, M., You, H., Matsuda, T., Bielska-Lasota, M., Storm, H., Tucker, T., Coleman, M., CoNCoRD Working Group (2015) Global surveillance of cancer survival 1995–2009: Analysis of individual data for 25676887 patients from 279 population-based registries in 67 countries (CoNCoRD-2). *The Lancet* 385: 977–1010.

Allen, P. and Jones, L. (2011) Increasing the diversity of health care providers. In *Understanding New Labour's Market Reforms of the English NHS* (ed. A. Dixon, N. Mays and L. Jones). London: The King's Fund.

Appleby, J. (2011) Does poor health justify NHS reform? *British Medical Journal* 342: d566.

Appleby, J., Baird, B., Thompson, J. and Jabbal, J. (2015) *The NHS under the Coalition Government, Part 2: NHS Performance.* London: The King's Fund.

Bevan, G. and Hamblin, R. (2009) Hitting and missing targets by ambulance services for emergency calls: effects of different systems of performance measurement within the UK. *Journal of the Royal Statistical Society* 172(1): 161–90.

Bevan, G. and Skellern, M. (2011) Does competition between hospitals improve clinical quality? A review of evidence from two eras of competition in the English NHS. *British Medical Journal* 343: d6470.

Bevan, G., Karanikolos, M., Exley, J., Nolte, E., Connolly, S. and Mays, N. (2014) *The Four Health Systems of the United Kingdom: How Do They Compare?* London: Health Foundation and Nuffield Trust.

Bijlsma, M., Meijer, A. and Shestalova, V. (n.d.) Vertical relationships between health insurers and healthcare providers. CPB Document 167. The Hague: Centraal Planbureau.

Björnberg, A. (2015) *Euro Health Consumer Index 2014 Report.* Health Consumer Powerhouse.

Bloom, N., Propper, C., Seiler, S. and Van Reenen, J. (2010) The impact of competition on management quality: evidence from public hospitals. NBER Working Paper 16032. Cambridge, MA: National Bureau of Economic Research.

Booth, P. (2008) The young held to ransom – a public choice analysis of the UK state pension system. *Economic Affairs* 28(1): 4–10.

Booth, P. and Niemietz, K. (2014) *Growing the UK Pension Pot: The Case for Privatisation.* Discussion Paper 56. London: Institute of Economic Affairs.

Breyer, F., Zweifel, P. and Kifmann, M. (2005) *Gesundheitsökonomik.* Berlin and Heidelberg: Springer.

Caley, M. and Sidhu, K. (2011) Estimating the future healthcare costs of an aging population in the UK: expansion of morbidity and the need for preventative care. *Journal of Public Health* 33(1): 117–22.

Cancer Research UK (2015) The 20 most common cancers in 2013. Cancer incidence statistics, dataset (http://www.cancerresearchuk.org/sites/default/files/cstream-node/inc_cases_mf_20.xls).

Canoy, M. and Sauter, W. (2009) Hospital mergers and the public interest: recent developments in the Netherlands. TILEC Discussion Paper 2009-035. Tilburg Law and Economics Center.

Cawston, T. and Corrie, C. (2013) *The Cost of Our Health: The Role of Charging in Healthcare.* Reform Ideas no. 9. London: Reform.

Charité Virchow Klinikum (n.d.) Wahlleistungen (http://www.gesundheitsstadt-berlin.de/charite-virchow-klinikum-920/).

Charlesworth, A., Davies, A. and Dixon, J. (2012) Reforming payment for health care in Europe to achieve better value. Research Report. London: Nuffield Trust.

Chiappori, P., Durand, F. and Geoffard, P. (1998) Moral hazard and the demand for physician services: first lessons from a French natural experiment. *European Economic Review* 42: 499–511.

Comparis (2016) Krankenkassen vergleichen und Geld sparen (https://www.comparis.ch/krankenkassen/default.aspx).

Cooper, Z., Gibbons, S., Jones, S. and McGuire, A. (2011) Does hospital competition save lives? Evidence from the English NHS patient choice reforms. *Economic Journal* 121: F228–60.

Cooper, Z., Gibbons, S., Jones, S. and McGuire, A. (2012) Does competition improve public hospitals' efficiency? Evidence from a quasi-experiment in the English National Health Service. CEP Discussion Paper 1125. London: Centre for Economic Performance.

Coulter, A. (2010) Do patients want a choice and does it work? *British Medical Journal* 341: c4989 (http://dx.doi.org/10.1136/bmj.c4989).

Crisp, N. (2011) *24 Hours to Save the NHS. The Chief Executive's Account of Reform 2000–2006*. Oxford University Press.

Daley, C. and Gubb, J. (2013) *Healthcare Systems: Switzerland*. London: Civitas.

Davis, J. and Tallis, R. (2013) *NHS SOS: How the NHS Was Betrayed – And How We Can Save It*. London: Oneworld Publications.

Davis, J., Lister, J. and Wrigley, D. (2015) *NHS for Sale: Myths, Lies and Deception*. London: Merlin Press.

Davis, K., Stremikis, K., Squires, D. and Schoen, C. (2014) *Mirror, Mirror, on the Wall. How the Performance of the U.S. Health Care System Compares Internationally. 2014 Update*. New York and Washington, DC: The Commonwealth Fund.

Dawson, D., Gravelle, H., Jacobs, R., Martin, S. and Smith, P. (2007) The effect of expanding patient choice of provider on waiting times: evidence from a policy experiment. *Health Economics* 16: 113–28.

Department of Health (2000) *The NHS Plan: A Plan for Investment, A Plan for Reform* (Cm 4818-I). London: The Stationery Office.

Department of Health (2009) Guidance on NHS patients who wish to pay for additional private care. Policy Document. London: Department of Health.

Die Linke (2011) Programm der Partei DIE LINKE. Beschluss des Parteitages der Partei DIE LINKE vom 21 bis 23 Oktober 2011 in Erfurt, bestätigt durch einen Mitgliederentscheid im Dezember 2011.

Dixon, A. and Robertson, R. (2011) Patient choice of hospital. In *Understanding New Labour's Market Reforms of the English NHS* (ed. A. Dixon, N. Mays and L. Jones). London: The King's Fund.

Drummond, M. and Towse, A. (2012) Is it time to reconsider the role of patient co-payments for pharmaceuticals in Europe? *European Journal of Health Economics* 13: 1–5.

Drummond, M., Jönsson, B., Rutten, F. and Stargardt, T. (2011) Reimbursement of pharmaceuticals: reference pricing versus health technology assessment. *European Journal of Health Economics* 12(3): 263–71.

El-Gingihy, Y. (2015) *How to Dismantle the NHS in 10 Easy Steps*. Winchester: Zero Books.

Ellis, O. (2013) The agony of choice. *British Medical Journal* 347: f5344 (http://dx.doi.org/10.1136/bmj.f5344).

Eurocare (2014) Survival of cancer patients in Europe. The EUROCARE-5 Study Section 1: Survival Analysis 2000–2007 (https://w3.iss.it/site/EU5Results/forms/SA0007.aspx).

European Commission (2013) Health and economics analysis for an evaluation of the public private partnerships in health care delivery across EU.

European Observatory on Health Care Systems (2000) Health care systems in transition: Switzerland. Target 19 – Research and knowledge for health.

Eurostat (2015) Amenable and preventable deaths statistics (http://ec.europa.eu/eurostat/statistics-explained/index.php/Amenable_and_preventable_deaths_statistics).

Farrar, S., Yi, D. and Boyle, S. (2011) Payment by results. In *Understanding New Labour's Market Reforms of the English NHS* (ed. A. Dixon, N. Mays and L. Jones). London: The King's Fund.

Feachem, R., Sekhri, N. and White, K. (2002) Getting more for their dollar: a comparison of the NHS with California's Kaiser Permanente. *British Medical Journal* 324: 135–43.

Felder, S. (2003) Kapitaldeckung in der gesetzlichen Krankenversicherung über den Risikostrukturausgleich. *Jahrbuch für Wirtschaftswissenschaften* 54(1): 60–72.

Felder, S. and Werblow, A. (2003) Swiss social health insurance: co-payments work. CESifo DICE Report 3/200343. Munich: CESifo Group.

Feldstein, M. (1995) Tax avoidance and the deadweight loss of the income tax. NBER Working Paper 5055. Cambridge, MA: National Bureau of Economic Research.

Feldstein, M. (1999) Prefunding medicare. Working Paper 6917. Cambridge, MA: National Bureau of Economic Research.

Fotaki, M. (2007) Patient choice on healthcare in England and Sweden: from quasi-market and back to market? A comparative analysis of failure in unlearning. *Public Administration* 85: 1059–75.

Gardiol, L., Geoffard, P. and Grandchamp, C. (2005) Separating selection and incentive effects in health insurance. PSE Working Paper 2005-38. Paris-Jourdan Sciences Economiques.

Gay, J., Paris, V., Devaux, M. and de Looper, M. (2011) Mortality amenable to health care in 31 OECD countries: estimates and methodological issues. OECD Health Working Papers 55. Paris: OECD.

Gaynor, M., Moreno-Serram, R. and Propper, C. (2011) Death by market power: reform, competition and patient outcomes in the National Health Service. Working Paper 10/242. Bristol: Centre for Market and Public Organisation at the University of Bristol.

Gerfin, M. and Schellhorn, M. (2005) Nonparametric bounds on the effect of deductibles in health care insurance on doctor visits – Swiss evidence. IZA Discussion Paper 1616. Bonn: Forschungsinstitut zur Zukunft der Arbeit.

Gershlick, B., Charlesworth, A. and Taylor, E. (2015) *Public attitudes to the NHS. An Analysis of Responses to Questions in the British Social Attitudes Survey.* London: The Health Foundation.

Godlee, F. (2007) The market has failed. *British Medical Journal* 335: 0.1 (http://dx.doi.org/10.1136/bmj.39413.597465.47).

Godlee, F. (2012) Why markets don't work in healthcare. *British Medical Journal* 344:e3300 (http://dx.doi.org/10.1136/bmj.e3300).

Green, D. (1985) *Working-Class Patients and the Medical Establishment. Self-Help in Britain from the Mid-Nineteenth Century to 1948.* Farnham: Gower Publishing.

Gregory, I. (2009) Comparisons between geographies of mortality and deprivation from the 1900s and 2001: spatial analysis of census and mortality statistics. *British Medical Journal* 339: 1–8.

Hacker, J. (1998) The historical logic of national health insurance: structure and sequence in the development of British, Canadian, and U.S. medical policy. *Studies in American Political Development* 12(Spring): 57–130.

Haidt, J. (2012) *The Righteous Mind. Why Good People Are Divided by Politics and Religion.* London: Penguin Books.

Ham, C., Smith, J. and Eastmure, E. (2011) *Commissioning Integrated Care in a Liberated NHS.* London: Nuffield Trust.

Ham, C., Baird, B., Gregory, S., Jabbal, J. and Alderwick, H. (2015) *The NHS under the Coalition Government*, Part 1: *NHS Reform.* London: The King's Fund.

Hannan, D. (2015) Stop complaining about the NHS. You're getting what you asked for. Conservative Home, 21 January.

Hauck, K. and Street, A. (2007) Do targets matter? A comparison of English and Welsh national health priorities. *Health Economics* 16: 275–90.

Hayes, N. (2012) Did we really want a National Health Service? Hospitals, patients and public opinions before 1948. *English Historical Review* 127(526): 625–61.

Higgins, J. (2007) Health policy: a new look at NHS commissioning. *British Medical Journal* 334(7583): 22–24.

Holst, J. (2010) Patient cost sharing: reforms without evidence. Theoretical considerations and empirical findings from industrialized countries. Discussion Paper, Wissenschaftszentrum Berlin für Sozialforschung, Forschungsschwerpunkt Bildung, Arbeit und Lebenschancen, Forschungsgruppe Public Health, SP I 2010-303.

Howes, A. (2015) *A National Health Service for Patients.* Policy Ideas. London: Civitas.

Hurst, J. and Williams, S. (2012) Can NHS hospitals do more with less? Research report. London: Nuffield Trust.

Jones, O. (2014) *The Establishment: And How They Get Away With It*. London: Allen Lane.

Joumard, I., André, C. and Nicq, C. (2010) Health care systems: efficiency and institutions. OECD Economics Department Working Papers 769. Paris: OECD.

Kan, M. and Suzuki, W. (2010) Effects of cost sharing on the demand for physician services in Japan: evidence from a natural experiment. *Japan and the World Economy* 22: 1–12.

Klein, R. (2003) The great transformation. Postscript in *Motivation, Agency and Public Policy. Of Knights and Knaves, Pawns and Queens* (J. Le Grand). Oxford University Press.

Kocsis, V., Koning, P. and Mot, E. (2012) Reconsidering government intervention in hospital bankruptcies: the case of the Netherlands (http://ssrn.com/abstract=2306992).

Lal, D. (2012) *Lost Causes: The Retreat from Classical Liberalism*. London: Biteback Publishing.

Le Grand, J. (2003) *Motivation, Agency and Public Policy. Of Knights and Knaves, Pawns and Queens*. Oxford University Press.

Leu, R., Rutten, F., Brouwer, W., Matter, P. and Rütschi, C. (2009) *The Swiss and Dutch Health Insurance Systems: Universal Coverage and Regulated Competitive Insurance Markets*. New York and Washington, DC: The Commonwealth Fund.

Mandelstam, M. (2007) *Betraying the NHS: Health Abandoned*. London: Jessica Kingsley Publishers.

Mason, A. (2005) Does the English NHS have a 'health benefit basket'? *European Journal of Health Economics* 6: S18–S23.

Mays, N., Dixon, A. and Jones, L. (2011) Return to the market: objectives and evolution of New Labour's market reforms. In *Understanding New Labour's Market Reforms of the English NHS* (ed. A. Dixon, N. Mays and L. Jones). London: The King's Fund.

Minford, P. and Wang, J. (2011) Public spending, taxation and economic growth – the evidence. In *Sharper Axes, Lower Taxes: Big Steps to a Smaller State* (ed. P. Booth). London: Institute of Economic Affairs.

Mosca, I. (2012) Evaluating reforms in the Netherlands' competitive health insurance system. *Eurohealth* 18(3): 7–10.

Niemietz, K. (2007) From Bismarck to Friedman. *Economic Affairs* 27(2): 83–87.

Niemietz, K. (2014) *Health Check: The NHS and Market Reforms.* Discussion Paper 54. London: Institute of Economic Affairs.

Niemietz, K. (2015a) Internal markets, management by targets, and quasi-markets: an analysis of health care reforms in the English NHS. *Economic Affairs* 35(1): 93–108.

Niemietz, K. (2015b) *What Are We Afraid Of? Universal Healthcare in Market-Orientated Health Systems.* Current Controversies Paper 50. London: Institute of Economic Affairs.

Niemietz, K. (2015c) *A Patient Approach. Putting the Consumer at the Heart of UK Healthcare.* Discussion Paper 64. London: Institute of Economic Affairs.

Niemietz, K. (2015d) *Diagnosis: Overrated. An Analysis of the Structural Flaws in the NHS.* Discussion Paper 66. London: Institute of Economic Affairs.

Niemietz, K. (2016) The UK health system – an international comparison of health outcomes. UK 2020 Health Paper 1. London: UK 2020.

Oberender, P., Hebborn, A. and Zerth, J. (2002) *Wachstumsmarkt Gesundheit.* Stuttgart: Lucius und Lucius.

OBR (2015) Fiscal sustainability report. Supporting documents: graphs and tables (http://budgetresponsibility.org.uk/fsr/fiscal-sustainability-report-june-2015/).

OECD (2006) OECD Reviews of Health Systems: Switzerland 2006, Paris: OECD Publishing.

OECD (2012) Coverage for health care. In *Health at a Glance: Europe 2012.* Paris: OECD Publishing.

OECD (2015) *Fiscal Sustainability of Health Systems. Bridging Health and Finance Perspectives.* Paris: OECD Publishing.

OECD Stats (2016) OECD database (http://stats.oecd.org/index.aspx?DataSetCode=HEALTH_STAT).

ONS (2012a) Mortality in England and Wales: average life span, 2010 (http://www.ons.gov.uk/ons/rel/mortality-ageing/mortality-in -england-and-wales/average-life-span/rpt-average-life-span.html ?format=print).

ONS (2012b) Mortality, 2010-based NPP Reference Volume (http://www .ons.gov.uk/ons/dcp171776_253938.pdf).

Player, S. and Leys, C. (2011) *The Plot against the NHS*. Pontypool: The Merlin Press.

Pollock, A. (2004) *NHS Plc: The Privatisation of Our Health Care*. London: Verso Books.

Pollock, A. (2011) Private finance initiatives during NHS austerity. *British Medical Journal* 342: d324.

Pollock, A. (forthcoming) *The End of the NHS*. London: Verso Books.

Pollock, A., Macfarlane, A. and Greener, I. (2012) Bad science concerning NHS competition is being used to support the controversial Health and Social Care Bill. LSE British Politics and Policy blog, London School of Economics.

Propper, C., Croxson, B. and Shearer, A. (2002) Waiting times for hospital admissions: the impact of GP fundholding. *Journal of Health Economics* 21: 227–52.

Propper, C., Burgess, S. and Green, K. (2004) Does competition between hospitals improve the quality of care? Hospital death rates and the NHS internal market. *Journal of Public Economics* 88: 1247–72.

Propper, C., Burgess, S. and Gossage, D. (2008) Competition and quality: evidence from the NHS internal market 1991–9. *Economic Journal* 118: 138–70.

Richards, M. (2010) Extent and causes of international variations in drug usage. A report for the Secretary of State for Health by Professor Sir Mike Richards CBE. UK Government.

Robson, W. (2002) Saving for health: prefunding health care for an older Canada. Health Papers 170. C. D. Howe Institute.

Rosen, B., Waitzberg, R. and Merkur, S. (2015) Israel. Health system review. Health Systems in Transition.

Roser, M. (2016) Life expectancy. Our World In Data (http://ourworldin data.org/data/population-growth-vital-statistics/life-expectancy/).

Schäfer, W., Kroneman, M., Boerma, W., van den Berg, M., Westert, G., Devillé, W. and van Ginneken, E. (2010) The Netherlands: health system review. *Health Systems in Transition* 12(1): 1–229.

Schellhorn, M. (2002a) A comparison of alternative methods to model endogeneity in count models: an application to the demand for health care and health insurance choice. Working Paper. Bonn: Institut Zukunft der Arbeit.

Schellhorn, M. (2002b) Auswirkungen wählbarer Selbstbehalte in der Krankenversicherung: Lehren aus der Schweiz? *Vierteljahrshefte zur Wirtschaftsforschung* 71(4): 411–26.

Schönfelder, B. and Wild, F. (2013) *Volkswirtschaftliche Wirkungen der Alterungsrückstellungen in der Privaten Kranken – und Pflegeversicherung. Ein Beitrag zur aktuellen Reformdiskussion.* Cologne: Wissenschaftliches Institut der PKV.

Schut, F. and van de Ven, W. (2011) Effects of purchaser competition in the Dutch health system: is the glass half full or half empty? *Health Economics, Policy and Law* 6: 109–23.

Schut, F., Sorbe, S. and Høj, J. (2013) Health care reform and long-term care in the Netherlands. Economics Department Working Paper 1010. Paris: OECD Publishing.

Seldon, A. (2004 [Originally 1990]) *The Virtues of Capitalism.* Indianapolis: Liberty Fund.

Siciliani, L., Moran, V. and Borowitz, M. (2014) Measuring and comparing health care waiting times in OECD countries. *Health Policy* 118: 292–303.

Smith, D. (2007) *Living with Leviathan: Public Spending, Taxes and Economic Performance.* London: Institute of Economic Affairs.

Smith, D. (2011) The changing economic role of government: past, present and prospective. In *Sharper Axes, Lower Taxes. Big Steps to a Smaller State* (ed. P. Booth). London: Institute of Economic Affairs.

Smith, J. and Curry, N. (2011) Commissioning. In *Understanding New Labour's Market Reforms of the English NHS* (ed. A. Dixon, N. Mays and L. Jones). London: The King's Fund.

Söderlund, N., Csaba, I., Gray, A., Milne, R. and Raftery, J. (1997) Impact of the NHS reforms on English hospital productivity: an analysis of the first three years. *British Medical Journal* 315: 1126–29.

Stabile, M. and Greenblatt, J. (2010) *Providing Pharmacare for an Aging Population: Is Prefunding the Solution?* IRPP Study 2. Montreal: Institute for Research on Public Policy.

Stadtspital Triemli (n.d.) Kosten und Tarife (https://www.stadt-zuer ich.ch/triemli/de/index/patienten_besucher/kosten.html).

Stroke Association (2016) *State of the Nation. Stroke Statistics*. London: Stroke Association.

Taylor, R. (2013) *God Bless the NHS: The Truth Behind the Current Crisis*. London: Faber and Faber.

Timmins, N. and Davies, E. (2015) *Glaziers and Window Breakers. The Role of the Secretary of State for Health, In Their Own Words*. London: The Health Foundation.

US Census Bureau (2013) Table HIB-4. Health Insurance Coverage Status and Type of Coverage by State All People: 1999 to 2012 (https://www.census.gov/data/tables/time-series/demo/health-insurance/historical-series/hib.html).

van de Ven, W., Beck, K., Buchner, F., Schokkaert, E., Schut, E., Shmueli, A. and Wasem, J. (2013) Preconditions for efficiency and affordability in competitive healthcare markets: are they fulfilled in Belgium, Germany, Israel, the Netherlands and Switzerland? *Health Policy* 109: 226–45.

Webster, C. (2002) *The National Health Service: A Political History*. Oxford University Press.

Werblow, A. (2002) Alles nur Selektion? Der Einfluss von Selbstbehalten in der Gesetzlichen Krankenversicherung. *Vierteljahrshefte zur Wirtschaftsforschung* 71(4): 427–36.

WHO (2015) *World Health Statistics 2015*. Geneva: World Health Organization.

ABOUT THE IEA

The Institute is a research and educational charity (No. CC 235 351), limited by guarantee. Its mission is to improve understanding of the fundamental institutions of a free society by analysing and expounding the role of markets in solving economic and social problems.

The IEA achieves its mission by:

- a high-quality publishing programme
- conferences, seminars, lectures and other events
- outreach to school and college students
- brokering media introductions and appearances

The IEA, which was established in 1955 by the late Sir Antony Fisher, is an educational charity, not a political organisation. It is independent of any political party or group and does not carry on activities intended to affect support for any political party or candidate in any election or referendum, or at any other time. It is financed by sales of publications, conference fees and voluntary donations.

In addition to its main series of publications the IEA also publishes a quarterly journal, *Economic Affairs*.

The IEA is aided in its work by a distinguished international Academic Advisory Council and an eminent panel of Honorary Fellows. Together with other academics, they review prospective IEA publications, their comments being passed on anonymously to authors. All IEA papers are therefore subject to the same rigorous independent refereeing process as used by leading academic journals.

IEA publications enjoy widespread classroom use and course adoptions in schools and universities. They are also sold throughout the world and often translated/reprinted.

Since 1974 the IEA has helped to create a worldwide network of 100 similar institutions in over 70 countries. They are all independent but share the IEA's mission.

Views expressed in the IEA's publications are those of the authors, not those of the Institute (which has no corporate view), its Managing Trustees, Academic Advisory Council members or senior staff.

Members of the Institute's Academic Advisory Council, Honorary Fellows, Trustees and Staff are listed on the following page.

The Institute gratefully acknowledges financial support for its publications programme and other work from a generous benefaction by the late Professor Ronald Coase.

Flaws and Ceilings – Price Controls and the Damage They Cause
Edited by Christopher Coyne and Rachel Coyne
Hobart Paperback 179; ISBN 978-0-255-36701-1; £12.50

Scandinavian Unexceptionalism: Culture, Markets and the Failure of Third-Way Socialism
Nima Sanandaji
Readings in Political Economy 1; ISBN 978-0-255-36704-2; £10.00

Classical Liberalism – A Primer
Eamonn Butler
Readings in Political Economy 2; ISBN 978-0-255-36707-3; £10.00

Federal Britain: The Case for Decentralisation
Philip Booth
Readings in Political Economy 3; ISBN 978-0-255-36713-4; £10.00

Forever Contemporary: The Economics of Ronald Coase
Edited by Cento Veljanovski
Readings in Political Economy 4; ISBN 978-0-255-36710-3; £15.00

Power Cut? How the EU Is Pulling the Plug on Electricity Markets
Carlo Stagnaro
Hobart Paperback 180; ISBN 978-0-255-36716-5; £10.00

Policy Stability and Economic Growth – Lessons from the Great Recession
John B. Taylor
Readings in Political Economy 5; ISBN 978-0-255-36719-6; £7.50

Breaking Up Is Hard To Do: Britain and Europe's Dysfunctional Relationship
Edited by Patrick Minford and J. R. Shackleton
Hobart Paperback 181; ISBN 978-0-255-36722-6; £15.00

In Focus: The Case for Privatising the BBC
Edited by Philip Booth
Hobart Paperback 182; ISBN 978-0-255-36725-7; £12.50

Islamic Foundations of a Free Society
Edited by Nouh El Harmouzi and Linda Whetstone
Hobart Paperback 183; ISBN 978-0-255-36728-8; £12.50

The Economics of International Development: Foreign Aid versus Freedom for the World's Poor
William Easterly
Readings in Political Economy 6; ISBN 978-0-255-36731-8; £7.50

Taxation, Government Spending and Economic Growth
Edited by Philip Booth
Hobart Paperback 184; ISBN 978-0-255-36734-9; £15.00

Other IEA publications

Comprehensive information on other publications and the wider work of the IEA can be found at www.iea.org.uk. To order any publication please see below.

Personal customers

Orders from personal customers should be directed to the IEA:

Clare Rusbridge
IEA
2 Lord North Street
FREEPOST LON10168
London SW1P 3YZ
Tel: 020 7799 8907. Fax: 020 7799 2137
Email: sales@iea.org.uk

Trade customers

All orders from the book trade should be directed to the IEA's distributor:

NBN International (IEA Orders)
Orders Dept.
NBN International
10 Thornbury Road
Plymouth PL6 7PP
Tel: 01752 202301, Fax: 01752 202333
Email: orders@nbninternational.com

IEA subscriptions

The IEA also offers a subscription service to its publications. For a single annual payment (currently £42.00 in the UK), subscribers receive every monograph the IEA publishes. For more information please contact:

Clare Rusbridge
Subscriptions
IEA
2 Lord North Street
FREEPOST LON10168
London SW1P 3YZ
Tel: 020 7799 8907, Fax: 020 7799 2137
Email: crusbridge@iea.org.uk